Don't Be Scared

Don't Be Scared is dedicated to all children and families cared for at Bristol Royal Hospital for Children and to the amazing teams of hospital staff who care for them.

Don't Be Scared

Above & Beyond
in aid of
Bristol Royal Hospital for Children

 *redcliffe*

First published in 2016 by Redcliffe Press Ltd., 81g Pembroke Road, Bristol BS8 3EA
www.redcliffepress.co.uk
info@redcliffepress.co.uk
in collaboration with Above & Beyond (Registered Charity No. 229945)

Text by Julia Donaldson and illustrations by Nick Sharratt for *Class Photograph* and *Question Time* taken from *Crazy Mayonnaisy Mum*. First published in 2004 by Macmillan Children's Books. Text copyright © Julia Donaldson 2004. Illustrations copyright © Nick Sharrat 2004.

Illustrations by Quentin Blake for *The Third Miracle* taken from *Matilda* by Roald Dahl, published by Jonathan Cape. Used by permission of The Random House Group Limited.

Text by Roald Dahl for *The Third Miracle* taken from *Matilda*, published by Jonathan Cape Ltd & Penguin.

Text by Carol Ann Duffy for *Don't Be Scared* and *Chocs* Copyright © Carol Ann Duffy. Reproduced by permission of the author c/o Rogers, Coleridge & White Ltd., 20 Powis Mews, London W11 1JN.

Text by Penelope Lively for *Next Term, We'll Mash You* taken from *Pack of Cards*, published by Penguin Ltd.

Illustrations by Nicola Bayley for *Next Term, We'll Mash You*. Original works copyright ©2013 by Nicola Bayley reproduced by kind permission of Nicola Bayley c/o Caroline Sheldon Literary Agency Ltd.

Text by Geraldine McCaughrean for *Sidecar* taken from *Puffin Post*, published by Puffin.

Text by Anne Fine for *You Don't Look Very Poorly* taken from *Crummy Mummy and Me*, published by Penguin.

Text by Michael Morpurgo and illustrations by Emma Chichester Clark for *The Best of Times*, published by Egmont.

Text by Anthony Horowitz for *The Double Eagle Has Landed* from *Guys Read: Thriller* by Jon Scieszka. Used by permission of HarperCollins Publishers

ISBN 978-1-908326-82-9
British Library Cataloguing-in-Publication Data
A catalogue record for this book is available from the British Library

Cover illustration and design by Nikola Ambros
Concept, design and typesetting by Nikola Ambros

Printed in the Czech Republic via Akcent Media

Contents

Thank You's

Don't Be Scared was the brainchild of Caro Ness who is also a contributor. We are very grateful to Caro for her passion for this project and for approaching so many contributors to make her vision, a children's book to raise funds for the children's hospital, a reality.

The anthology has been beautifully designed by Nikola Ambros who has consistently shown commitment to this project above and beyond the call of duty. It is thanks to Redcliffe Press that we have been able to bring *Don't Be Scared* to publication, and we are extremely grateful to John Sansom and Clara Hudson for their belief in and support for this book.

Last but not least, many of our most respected children's authors and illustrators have generously contributed their work to help Above & Beyond raise funds for Bristol Royal Hospital for Children, and we would like to warmly thank every single one of them.

Contributors

Nicola Bayley, Ellen Beier, Quentin Blake, Herbie Brennan, Raymond Briggs, Mike Brownlow, Romi Caron, Emma Chichester Clark, Wendy Cope, Roald Dahl, Kate Daubney, Julia Donaldson, Carol Ann Duffy, Rose Fay, Anne Fine, Michael Foreman, Anthony Horowitz, Michael Jecks, Andrew Joyce, Satoshi Kitamura, Penelope Lively, Jacqui Mair, Alexander McCall Smith, Geraldine McCaughrean, Michael Morpurgo, Caro Ness, Hiawyn Oram, Michael Rosen, Tony Ross, Adrienne Salgado, Nick Sharratt, Yuliya Somina, Sam Usher, Martin Waddell, Sholto Walker, Jacqueline Wilson

The Charity

Above & Beyond is the charity that raises funds for all Bristol's city centre hospitals including Bristol children's hospital. They fundraise to improve the hospital environment, for innovative research, for staff training and support and to provide state-of-the-art equipment. They fund projects that make a real difference to patient care, above and beyond what the NHS can provide. When patients, their families and friends want to say thank you for the care they have received at the hospitals, they come to Above & Beyond.

Above & Beyond
The Abbot's House, Blackfriars, Bristol BS1 2NZ
Tel: 0117 927 7120
Email: hello@aboveandbeyond.org.uk
Web: www.aboveandbeyond.org.uk
Registered Charity No: 229945

Foreword

At hospitals' charity Above & Beyond, we work closely with our inspirational donors and supporters to raise funds for all Bristol's city centre hospitals including Bristol Royal Hospital for Children. The children's hospital provides an excellent local service treating Bristol's children, but it also provides specialist care for children across the South West and nationally, even internationally.

We believe every child deserves the very best care in the very best surroundings and that it's also important for children in hospital to have the chance to play and develop. That's why we are delighted that so many of Britain's best-loved writers and illustrators have generously donated their stories, poems and illustrations for children to this anthology.

Their support, and yours, will help us raise funds for all those things that are above and beyond what the NHS can provide in the children's hospital: from state-of-the-art life-saving equipment to an endless supply of glitter, glue and craft materials to help entertain and distract our very sick children.

Don't Be Scared will make a difference to so many children in hospital and to their families. We hope the book will also bring you and those you read it to, the magic of childhood and a child's unique way of seeing the world to which these wonderfully talented contributors have very special access. We hope you enjoy reading it.

Drummond Forbes
Chairman

Is Anybody There?

(being a fictional discourse on matters moral,
philosophical and supernatural)

Written by Herbie Brennan
Illustrations by Yuliya Somina

L ip was the one who suggested a séance. She was coming down off something and was jittery bored. Tar and Wit, the creepy twins, weighed in at once: they were always up for something spooky – Tar claimed they'd once resurrected their dead grandfather using magic from an old book. Heather was curled around Samson on the rickety old couch, so neither of them cared. Jeanette said, "We can't have a séance – we don't have a medium." Then, because she liked making stupid puns, she added, "Not even a happy medium."

"Don't need one," Tar said; or possibly Wit. It was difficult to tell them apart. They both wore suits – suits! – shirts and ties of the same colour. It was all part of the thing they had about wanting to change the world. They thought suits would help people take them seriously.

Jeanette, who was terribly, terribly pretty and terribly, terribly superior, said, "Of course we do," in an exaggerated, upper-class drawl.

Lip said, "We can use a glass."

They all looked at her. "It's simple, duh!" Lip said, shaking her head in mock astonishment. "You cut up twenty-seven squares of paper, one for every letter of the alphabet; and then two more, for yes and no."

Jeanette was looking at her blankly. "You mean we write all twenty-seven letters of the alphabet on squares of paper?"

"That's what I just said."

Samson disentangled himself briefly from Heather. "Only twenty-six," he said. Jeanette transferred her blank look from Lip. Samson shrugged. "Letters in the alphabet." Then he went back to snogging Heather.

"Whatever," Lip said. She grinned abruptly. "Then, when you've done that, you spread them out in a circle on a table —"

"Like a card table?" Wit asked. Although he'd been named for the philosopher Wittgenstein, he was the practical one of the twins, never afraid to ask questions.

"No, it needs to have a polished surface. Then you get a glass, like an ordinary tumbler, and you put it upside down in the middle of the circle. Then everybody gathers round and puts one forefinger on the rim of the glass. Then somebody asks 'Is anybody there?' and the glass will start to move of its own accord."

"What's the point of that?" Heather pushed Samson's octopus arms away, sat up and straightened her skirt.

"It spells out messages," Lip told her.

"Yes, but only because we'd be pushing it."

Tar said thoughtfully, "No we wouldn't, not if we all had our fingers round the rim. If everybody's pushing evenly, the glass wouldn't move at all, and if one of us was pushing for a lark, the others would feel it."

"It's the spirits who push it," Lip said in sepulchral tones, wiggling her fingers.

"Perhaps it is and perhaps it isn't," Wit told her. "But it's certainly worth a scientific experiment."

They discussed the question of the table for a while and decided to use the priceless, highly-polished, Victorian antique dining table in Jeanette's parents' Chelsea home, a decision facilitated by the fact that Jeanette's parents were currently in Cannes.

They all congregated in Chelsea that evening and Jeanette, who was very well brought up, served them small glasses of her father's sherry. Samson pretended to get tipsy until Heather gave him The Look and he calmed down again. "I've made the paper squares, and given the maid a night off, so we can start right in," Jeanette said.

Jeanette's paper squares were impressive. She'd printed the alphabet from her laptop then cut out each letter carefully using pinking shears. The result was almost professional.

"Do we need to draw the curtains and switch off the lights?" Tar asked as they began to arrange the letters in a circle. The dining room had heavy velvet curtains that stretched from floor to ceiling. With them drawn and the lights out, the room would be in darkness.

"The curtains – yes," Lip said. "We don't want anybody peering at us through the window. But we'll keep some lights on, otherwise we won't see what we're doing."

Jeanette produced a cut-crystal whisky tumbler and upended it in the middle of the circle. They took their seats and stared at it. "What do we do now?" Heather asked. They all turned to look at Lip, who'd suggested the whole business in the first place and was thus considered an expert.

"We must connect with the glass," Lip said confidently. "Each of you put a forefinger on the rim. Lightly."

Forefingers were hesitantly extended, one by one. From above, the glass took on the appearance of a wheel hub, with humans ranged around the rim.

After a moment, Tar echoed Heather's earlier question: "What do we do now?"

"We wait," Lip said.

They waited. When nothing happened, Wit said, frowning, "Shouldn't someone be asking 'Is anybody there?'?"

Tar frowned. "I don't think we should ask 'Is anybody there?' That sounds as if we're inviting just any old spook to make contact."

"What would you suggest?" his twin asked soberly.

"I think we should say, 'Is somebody there?'"

"I think 'Is anybody there?' is the traditional thing to say," Jeanette told them. As faces turned towards her, she added defensively, "There's a book on Spiritualism in my father's library."

"I think we should stick to the traditional thing," Samson said quickly. He had a nervous look about him.

"So do I." Heather always agreed with Samson when she wasn't fighting him off.

Tar shrugged. "All right," he said. He elevated his gaze so that his nose was at an angle to the ceiling and intoned loudly, "Is anybody there?"

The glass trembled.

"My God!" squeaked Heather, snatching her finger away.

"You must keep your finger on the glass," Lip told her sternly. Slowly, reluctantly, Heather put it back.

Nothing much happened for more than five minutes, a very long time when you're sitting in a circle with your finger on a glass.

"Will I say it again?" Tar asked softly.

Lip nodded. "Yes." They were both whispering, as if speaking in a cathedral.

"Is anybody there?" Tar intoned again. The glass shuddered, moved a definite inch, then stopped.

"It moved!" Samson said unnecessarily. His eyes were wide. The glass shot abruptly across the table top, halting near the circle of letters. Heather's finger came off it, but she put it quickly back again. The glass tipped, righted itself, then began to move slowly around the circle of letters, pausing at each one like a dog sniffing lampposts.

"Oh my God, oh my God," Heather murmured. She looked thoroughly frightened. Samson, who was seated beside her, reached out to hold her free hand.

"Ask again," Wit told Tar quietly.

"Is anybody there?" Tar asked for the third time.

The glass moved swiftly and directly the square of paper that showed the word YES. Then it moved back to the centre of the circle and sat there, trembling slightly as if in anticipation.

For a long moment, nobody said anything, then everybody began to talk at once.

"What do we do now?"

"You were pushing, Lip – I felt you."

"I don't think we should go on with this."

"Of course I wasn't. If anybody was, you were."

"I felt a spirit presence."

This last remark, from Jeanette, stopped everybody short. Heather said hesitantly, "Don't joke about things like that, Jeanie."

"I wasn't joking," Jeanette said flatly. "I felt something. Like a cold wind."

"Maybe Wit farted," Samson suggested, grinning.

Heather rounded on him savagely. "Shut up! You always try to make fun of anything you don't understand!"

"Sorry," Samson muttered grumpily.

Lip said to Tar, "Ask if it has any message for us. The spirit, or whatever it is."

"No, don't do that," Heather put in quickly. "It might tell us something bad."

"Isn't that the whole point?" asked Wit. He shook his head. "Not that it will tell us something bad, but that it will tell us something. We have to take our chances about what it is."

"Why don't we," suggested Jeanette, "ask who it is? Then we can get some idea if the message is likely to be good or bad."

"Excellent idea," said Wit. He looked around. "Everybody happy with that?" Except for Lip and Tar, everybody avoided his eyes, which he took as a sign of assent. He nodded to Tar. "Go ahead."

Tar turned towards the trembling glass. "Would you like to spell out your name for us?" he asked politely.

The glass rushed from letter to letter. The name it spelled was S-A-T-A-N.

"Do you think it really was Satan?" Wit asked his brother as they trudged through the empty back-streets en route home. The others had bolted for their own homes, except Jeanette, of course, who was already home and had nowhere else to go. But she'd burned the letters in the dining room fireplace, put the glass into the dishwasher, and found a large, free-standing crucifix which she set in the middle of the table.

"What, the supreme embodiment of universal evil, responsible for all the woes and wars of this world, the Antichrist, the Adversary, Lucifer, the Devil, Old Nick, the Father of Lies, pushing Jeanette's father's whisky glass about? I don't think so." He sniffed, not to emphasise his scepticism, but because the damp night air was getting to him. "But I suppose it's possible."

"We can always find out."

Tar arched an eyebrow. "Use the Lemegeton?"

"That's what I was thinking," Wit told him. The Lemegeton was an old book of magic they'd discovered in a junk shop. They'd used it to resurrect their dead grandfather for a while – an operation that proved tricky, although it turned out all right in the end – but it was really designed to call up the devil.

"Yes, okay," Tar said. "When we get home?"

"That's what I was thinking," Wit said again.

***

They chalked their magic circle in the cellar, as they'd done before, drew the same sigils and added nutmeg to the incense. But this time they drew a triangle outside the circle since they were calling up Satan, who might well be dangerous, and not their old grandfather, who was fairly harmless.

"Do you think he'll be prepared to communicate?" Tar asked.

"The book says he will," Wit told him.

"In words?"

"How else would he communicate?"

Tar shrugged. "He talked to Tartini in music." The twins were fearfully intelligent and well-educated. The eighteenth century composer Tartini dreamed the devil played a violin sonata for him, wrote it down when he woke up, and became famous as a result. "I was listening to Vanessa Mae play it on YouTube just last week."

"He'll talk to us in words," Wit said confidently. "Or possibly telepathy."

They lit the candles and the incense and Wit, who read things well, began the evocation. The last time they'd substituted Grandpa's name, but this time they stuck to the original, Lucifuge Rofocal, which was what the Lemegeton called Satan. After a while, a misty form began to manifest inside the triangle. As Wit finished the evocation, it solidified into an ugly, leather-skinned humanoid with enormous bat wings, horns and an arrow-head tail. The teeth would have done justice to a vampire. "In fair and pleasant form," Wit told it hurriedly, reading from the book.

The creature transformed into a plump, balding middle-aged man in a badly cut business suit. "Will anybody ever love me for what I am?" he sighed.

"Are you Satan?" Tar asked.

"That is one of my many aliases," Satan admitted, then added bewilderingly, "and functions." He smiled benignly. "I don't suppose I can trick you into letting me out of this triangle? No, thought not – you're such intelligent twins."

Tar, who liked to cut to the chase, said, "We held a séance earlier today and when we asked was anybody there the glass spelled out Satan. Was that you?"

"What, me – the supreme embodiment of universal evil, responsible for all the woes and wars of this world, the Antichrist, the Adversary, Lucifer, the Devil, Old Nick, the Father of Lies, pushing some cheap tumbler about? I don't think so."

"Actually it was cut crystal," Tar told him. "But I take your point. So it wasn't you?"

Satan sniffed. "It wasn't even a spirit. Is this really all you called me up to ask?"

"What else should we ask you?" Wit put in.

"Oh, you know, sophisticated philosophical questions about the nature of good and evil, the paradox of a benign deity permitting me to exist – that sort of thing. We could have one of those very cool discussions Faust had with Mephistopheles; who was me, incidentally, whatever Goethe claimed."

But Tar was not to be diverted by frivolities. "What do you mean, it wasn't even a spirit?"

Satan sighed so loudly the sound was almost camp. "None of those séance things are spirits, not the glass moving, nor the table tipping, nor the levitating trumpets, nor the taps nor the raps nor the voices in the air. They're all created by the group mind of the sitters."

"But they claim to be spirits," Tar protested.

Satan shrugged. "Mr. Pickwick claimed to be a fat cheerful bloke who lived in Victorian times, but that doesn't make him any less a fictional character."

Wit found himself being dragged into the discussion, despite his practical streak. "Fictional characters can only do what their authors want them to do."

Satan gave him a withering look. "You've obviously never discussed that with an author." He straightened his jacket impatiently. "Look, is this really the only thing you wanted to ask me? Whether I pushed a glass about at your séance? If it is, I'd rather like to be going. Wars to start, famines to supervise, superbugs to evolve, babies to eat... that sort of thing."

Tar ignored him. "So it was our minds that pushed the glass?"

"Not directly," Satan admitted. "It was your minds that created the entity that pushed the glass."

"Really?" Tar breathed.

"Been doing it for centuries," Satan said easily. "Human minds are very creative, even when their owners don't know what they're doing.

And not just séance spirits either: ghosts... gods... even... " He glanced upwards slyly. "... the big fellow Himself."

"The big fellow Himself? You mean we created God?"

"Of course. But that's the best-kept secret in the universe."

"What about —?" Tar began.

Wit finished his sentence for him, something that often happened between the twins. "— you?"

Satan looked suddenly uncomfortable. "Me?" he echoed. He coughed. "Not sure I follow —"

"Have our minds created you?" Tar asked bluntly.

"Here and now," Wit added vindictively.

"No, of course not," Satan blustered. "Can't you see me standing here as solid as —?"

But in fact he was no longer as solid as any metaphor he might have hit on. His voice was fading to an increasingly distant reverberation, his form taking on the indistinct appearance of steam. Tar and Wit watched curiously as he faded into nothingness with an audible pop.

"We made him up," Tar said, his eyes wide.

"You know what this means?" Wit told him. It was phrased as a question, but they both knew it was actually a leading statement. Tar waited. "It means we can change everything. Once we get people to take responsibility for the entities they create, there will be no more intolerance, no more bigotry, no more crusades, no more holy wars."

"No more false hopes, no more exploitation of the planet, no more messages from God telling people what they want to hear to justify their actions," Tar added.

"Let's start tonight," Wit said with all the energy and enthusiasm of youth.

They broke the circle, read the licence to depart (just in case) then went out together to save the world.

A Blind Man Catches a Bird

Written by Alexander McCall Smith
Illustration by Kate Daubney

A young man married a woman whose brother was blind. The young man was eager to get to know his new brother-in-law and so he asked him if he would like to go hunting with him. "I cannot see," the blind man said. "But you can help me see when we are out hunting together. We can go."

The young man led the blind man off into the bush. At first they followed a path that he knew and it was easy for the blind man to tag on behind the other. After a while though, they went off into thicker bush, where the trees grew closely together and there were many places for the animals to hide. The blind man now held on to the arm of the sighted brother-in-law and told him many things about the sounds that they heard around them. Because he had no sight, he had a great ability to interpret the noises made by the animals in the bush.

"There are warthogs round," he would say. "I can hear their noises over there."

Or, "That bird is preparing to fly. Listen to the sound of its wings unfolding."

To the brother-in-law, these sounds were meaningless, and he was most impressed at the blind man's ability to understand the bush although it must have been for him one great darkness.

They walked on for several hours, until they reached a place where they could set their traps. The blind man followed the other's advice and put his trap in a place where birds might come for water. The other man put his trap a short distance away, taking care to disguise it so that no bird would know that it was there. He did not bother to disguise the blind man's trap, as it was hot and he was eager to get home to his new wife. The blind man thought that he had disguised his trap, but he did not see that he had failed to do so and any bird could tell that there was a trap there.

They returned to their hunting place the next day. The blind man was excited at the prospect of having caught something, and the young man had to tell him to keep quiet, or he would scare all the animals away. Even before they reached the traps, the blind man was able to tell that they had caught something.

"I can hear birds. There are birds in the traps."

When he reached his trap, the young man saw that he had caught a small bird. He took it out of his trap and put it in a pouch that he had brought with him. Then the two of them walked towards the blind man's trap.

"There is a bird in it," he said to the blind man. "You have caught a bird too."

As he spoke, he felt himself filling with jealousy. The blind man's bird was marvellously coloured, as if it had flown through a rainbow and been stained by the colours. The feathers from a bird such as that would make a fine present for his new wife, but the blind man had a wife too and she would also want the feathers.

The young man bent down and took the blind man's bird from the trap. Then, quickly, substituting his own bird, he passed it to the blind man and put the coloured bird in his own pouch.

"Here is your bird," he said to the blind man. "You may put it in your pouch."

The blind man reached out for the bird and took it. He felt it for a moment, his fingers passing over the wings and breast. Then, without saying anything, he put the bird in his pouch and they began the trip home.

On the way home, the two men stopped to rest under a broad tree. As they sat there, they talked about many things. The young man was impressed by the wisdom of the blind man, who knew a great deal, although he could see nothing at all.

"Why do people fight with one another?" he asked the blind man. It was a question which had always troubled him and he wondered if the blind man could give him an answer.

The blind man said nothing for a few moments, but it was clear to the young man that he was thinking. Then the blind man raised his head, and it seemed to the young man as if his unseeing eyes were staring right into his soul. Quietly he gave his answer.

"Men fight because they do to each other what you have just done to me."

The words shocked the young man and made him ashamed. He tried to think of a response, but none came. Rising to his feet, he fetched his pouch, took out the brightly coloured bird and gave it back to the blind man.

The blind man took the bird, felt over it with his fingers, and smiled.

"Do you have any other questions for me?" he asked.

"Yes," said the young man. "How do men become friends after they have fought?"

The blind man smiled again.

"They do what you have just done," he said. "That's how they become friends again."

Question Time

From *Crazy Mayonnaisy Mum* by Julia Donaldson
Illustration by Nick Sharratt

How many books have you written?
Have you been writing for years?
Where do you get all the paper?
Where do you get your ideas?

Do you get bumps on your fingers?
Do you get aches in your wrist?
Please can I go to the toilet?
Did you write Oliver Twist?

I've got a book about spiders.
I've got a cut on my knee.
I've got an aunt who speaks German.
Gemma keeps tickling me.

Are you quite old? Are you famous?
Are you a millionaire?
I wasn't putting my hand up –
I was just twiddling my hair.

How many plays have you written?
Do you write one every day?
Do you ... oh dear, I've forgotten
What I was going to say.

Will you be staying to dinner?
Will you go home on the bus?
How many poems have you written?
Will you write one about us?

Class Photograph

From *Crazy Mayonnaisy Mum* by Julia Donaldson
Illustration by Nick Sharratt

Everyone's smiling, grinning, beaming,
Even Clare Biggs who was really scheming
How she was going to get revenge
On the ex-best friend, Selina Penge
(front row, third left, with her hair in wisps)
For stealing her salt and vinegar crisps.

And Martin Layton-Smith is beaming,
Though he was almost certainly dreaming
Of warlock warriors in dripping caves
Sending mindless orcs to their gruesome graves.
(Next to him, Christopher Jordan's dream
Has something to do with a football team.)

And Ann-Marie Struthers is sort of beaming,
Though a minute ago her eyes were streaming
Because she'd been put in the second back row
And separated from Jennifer Snow.
And Jennifer Snow is beaming too,
Though Miss Bell wouldn't let her go to the loo.

And Miss Bell, yes even Miss Bell is beaming,
Though only just now we'd heard her screaming
At the boy beside her, Robert Black,
Who kept on peeling his eyelids back
And making a silly hooting noise
(Though he said that was one of the other boys).

Eve Rice is doing her best at beaming.
Yes, Eve is reasonably cheerful seeming,
Though I think she was jealous because Ruth Chubb
Had – at last! – let me into their special club.
(In order to join the club, said Ruth,
You had to have lost at least one tooth.)

And look that's me, and my teeth are gleaming
Around my new gap, yes I'm really beaming.

The Third Miracle

From *Matilda* by Roald Dahl
Illustrations by Quentin Blake

T he next day was Thursday, and that, as the whole of Miss Honey's class knew, was the day on which the Headmistress would take charge of the first lesson after lunch.

In the morning Miss Honey said to them, "One or two of you did not particularly enjoy the last occasion when the Headmistress took the class, so let us all try to be especially careful and clever today. How are your ears, Eric, after your last encounter with Miss Trunchbull?"

"She stretched them," Eric said. "My mother said she's positive they are bigger than they were."

"And Rupert," Miss Honey said, "I am glad to see you didn't lose any of your hair after last Thursday."

"My head was jolly sore afterwards," Rupert said.

"And you Nigel," Miss Honey said, "do please try not to be smart-aleck with the Headmistress today. You were really quite cheeky to her last time."

"I hate her," Nigel said.

"Try not to make it so obvious," Miss Honey said. "It doesn't pay. She's a very strong woman. She has muscles like steel ropes."

"I wish I was grown up," Nigel said. "I'd knock her flat."

"I doubt you would," Miss Honey said. "No one has ever got the better of her yet."

"What will she be testing us on this afternoon?" a small girl asked.

"Almost certainly the three times table," Miss Honey said. "That's what you are all meant to have learned this past week. Make sure you know it."

Lunch came and went.

After lunch, the class reassembled. Miss Honey stood at one side of the room. They all sat silent, apprehensive, waiting. And then, like some giant of doom, the enormous Trunchbull strode into the room in her green breeches and cotton smock. She went straight to her jug of water and lifted it up by the handle and peered inside.

"I am glad to see," she said, "that there are no slimy creatures in my drinking water this time. If there had been then something exceptionally unpleasant would have happened to every single member of this class. And that includes you, Miss Honey."

The class remained silent and very tense. They had learnt a bit about this tigress by now and nobody was about to take any chances.

"Very well," boomed the Trunchbull. "Let us see how well you know your three-times table. Or to put it another way, let us see how badly Miss Honey has taught you the three-times table." The Trunchbull was standing in front of the class, legs apart, hands on hips, scowling at Miss Honey who stood silent to one side.

Matilda, sitting motionless at her desk in the second row, was watching things very closely.

"You!" the Trunchbull shouted, pointing a finger the size of a rolling-pin at a boy called Wilfred. Wilfred was on the extreme right of the front row. "Stand up you!" she shouted at him.

Wilfred stood up.

"Recite the three-times table backwards!" the Trunchbull barked.

"Backwards?" stammered Wilfred. "But I haven't learnt it backwards."

"There you are!" cried the Trunchbull, triumphant. "She's taught you nothing! Miss Honey, why have you taught them absolutely nothing at all in the last week?"

"That is not true, Headmistress," Miss Honey said. "They have all learnt their three-times table. But I see no point in teaching it to them backwards. There is little point in teaching anything backwards. The whole object of life, Headmistress, is to go forwards. I venture to ask whether even you, for example, can spell a simple word like wrong backwards straight away. I very much doubt it."

"Don't you get impertinent with me, Miss Honey!" the Trunchbull snapped, then she turned back to the unfortunate Wilfred. "Very well, boy," she said. "Answer me this. I have seven apples, seven oranges and seven bananas. How many pieces of fruit do I have altogether? Hurry up! Get on with it! Give me the answer!"

"That's adding up!" Wilfred cried. "That isn't the three-times table!"

"You blithering idiot!" shouted the Trunchbull. "You festering gumboil! You fleabitten fungus! That is the three-times table. You have three separate lots of fruit and each lot has seven pieces. Three sevens are twenty-one. Can't you see that, you stagnant cesspool? I'll give you one more chance. I have eight coconuts, eight monkey nuts and eight nutty little idiots like you. How many nuts do I have altogether? Answer me quickly."

Poor Wilfred was properly flustered. "Wait!" he cried. "Please wait! I've got to add up eight coconuts and eight monkey nuts ..." He started counting on his fingers.

"You bursting blister!" yelled the Trunchbull. "You moth-eaten maggot! This is not adding up! This is multiplication! The answer is three eights! Or is it eight threes? Tell me that you mangled little wurzel and look sharp about it!"

By now Wilfred was far too frightened and bewildered even to speak.

In two strides the Trunchbull was beside him, and by some amazing gymnastic trick, it may have been judo or karate, she flipped the back of Wilfred's legs with one of her feet so that the boy shot up off the ground and turned a somersault in the air. But halfway through the somersault she caught him by the ankle and held him dangling upside-down like a plucked chicken in a shop-window.

"Eight threes," the Trunchbull shouted, swinging Wilfred from side to side by his ankle, "eight threes is the same as three eights and three eights are twenty-four! Repeat that!"

At exactly that moment Nigel, at the other end of the room, jumped to his feet and started pointing excitedly at the blackboard and screaming, "The chalk! The chalk! Look at the chalk! It's moving all on its own!"

So hysterical and shrill was Nigel's scream that everyone in the place, including the Trunchbull, looked up at the blackboard. And there, sure enough, a brand-new piece of chalk was hovering near the grey-black writing surface of the blackboard.

"It's writing something!" screamed Nigel. "The chalk is writing something!"

And indeed it was.

Agatha

"What the blazes is this!" yelled the Trunchbull. It had shaken her to see her own first name being written like that by an invisible hand. She dropped Wilfred on to the floor.

Then she yelled at nobody in particular, "Who's doing this? Who's writing it?"

The chalk continued to write.

Agatha, this is Magnus
This is Magnus

Everyone in the place heard the gasp that came from the Trunchbull's throat. "No!" she cried, "It can't be! It can't be Magnus!"

It is Magnus
And you'd better believe it

Miss Honey, at the side of the room glanced swiftly at Matilda. The child was sitting very straight at her desk, the head held high, the mouth compressed, the eyes glittering like two stars.

Agatha, give my Jenny back her house
For some reason everyone now looked at the Trunchbull. The woman's face had turned white, as snow, her mouth was opening and shutting like a halibut out of water and giving out a series of strangled gasps.
Give my Jenny her wages
Give my Jenny the house
Then get out of here.
if you don't, I will come and get you
I will come and get you
Like you got me.
I am watching you
Agatha

The chalk stopped writing. It hovered for a few moments, then suddenly it dropped to the floor with a tinkle and broke in two.

Wilfred, who had managed to resume his seat in the front row, screamed, "Miss Trunchull has fallen down! Miss Trunchbull is on the floor!"

This was the most sensational bit of news of all and the entire class jumped up out of their seats to have a really good look. And there she was, the huge figure of the Headmistress, stretched full-length on her back across the floor, out for the count.

Miss Honey ran forward and knelt beside the prostrate giant. "She's fainted!" she cried. "She's out cold! Someone go and fetch the matron at once." Three children ran out of the room.

Nigel, always ready for action, leapt up and seized the big jug of water. "My father says cold water is the best way to wake up someone who's fainted," he said, and with that he tipped the entire contents of the jug over the Trunchbull's head. No one, not even Miss Honey, protested.

As for Matilda, she continued to sit motionless at her desk. She was feeling curiously elated. She felt as though she had touched something that was not quite of this world, the highest point of the heavens, the farthest star. She had felt most wonderfully the power surging up behind her eyes, gushing like a warm fluid inside her skull, and her eyes had become scorching hot, hotter than ever before, and things had come bursting out of her eye-sockets and then the piece of chalk had lifted itself up and had begun to write. It seemed as though she had hardly done anything, it had all been so simple.

The school matron, followed by five teachers, three women and two men, came rushing into the room.

"By golly, somebody's floored her at last!" cried one of the men, grinning. "Congratulations, Miss Honey!"

"Who threw the water over her?" asked the matron.

"I did," said Nigel proudly.

"Good for you," another teacher said. "Shall we get some more?"

"Stop that," the matron said. "We must carry her up to the sick-room."

It took all five teachers and the matron to lift the enormous woman and stagger with her out of the room.

Miss Honey said to the class, "I think you'd all better go out to the playground and amuse yourselves until the next lesson." Then she turned and walked over to the blackboard and carefully wiped out all the chalk writing.

The children began filing out of the classroom. Matilda started to go with them, but as she passed Miss Honey she paused and her twinkling eyes met the teacher's eyes and Miss Honey ran forward and gave the tiny child a great big hug and a kiss.

Don't Be Scared

Written by Carol Ann Duffy
Illustration by Michael Foreman

The dark is only a blanket
for the moon to put on her bed.

The dark is a private cinema
for the movie dreams in your head.

The dark is a little black dress
to show off the sequin stars.

The dark is the wooden hole
behind the strings of happy guitars.

The dark is a jeweller's velvet cloth
where children sleep like pearls.

The dark is a spool of film
to photograph boys and girls,
so smile in your sleep in the dark.

Don't be scared.

Next Term, We'll Mash You

From *Pack of Cards* by Penelope Lively

Illustrations by Nicola Bayley

I nside the car it was quiet, the noise of the engine even and subdued, the air just the right temperature, the windows tight-fitting. The boy sat on the back seat, a box of chocolates, unopened, beside him, and a comic, folded. The trim Sussex landscape flowed past the windows: cows, white-fenced fields, highly-priced period houses. The sunlight was glassy, remote as a coloured photograph. The backs of the two heads in front of him swayed with the motion of the car.

His mother half-turned to speak to him. "Nearly there now, darling."

The father glanced downwards at his wife's wrist. "Are we all right for time?"

"Just right. Nearly twelve."

"I could do with a drink. Hope they lay something on."

"I'm sure they will. The Wilcoxes say they're awfully nice people. Not really the schoolmaster-type at all, Sally says."

The man said, "He's an Oxford chap."

"Is he? You didn't say."

"Mmm."

"Of course, the fees are that much higher than the Seaford place."

"Fifty quid or so. We'll have to see."

The car turned right, between white gates and high, dark, tight-clipped hedges. The whisper of the road under the tyres changed to the crunch of gravel. The child, staring sideways, read black lettering on a white board: *St Edward's Preparatory School. Please Drive Slowly.* He shifted on the seat, and the leather sucked at the bare skin under his knees, stinging.

The mother said, "It's a lovely place. Those must be the playing-fields. Look, darling, there are some of the boys." She clicked open her handbag, and sun caught her mirror and flashed in the child's eyes; the comb went through her hair and he saw the grooves it left, neat as distant ploughing.

"Come on, then, Charles, out you get."

The building was red brick, early nineteenth century, spreading out long arms in which windows glittered blackly. Flowers, trapped in neat beds, were alternate red and white. They went up the steps, the man, the woman, and the child two paces behind.

The woman, the mother, smoothing down a skirt that would be ridged from sitting, thought: I like the way they've got the maid all done up properly. The little white apron and all that. She's foreign, I suppose. Au pair. Very nice. If he comes here there'll be Speech Days and that kind of thing. Sally Wilcox says it's quite dressy – she got that cream linen coat for coming down here. You can see why it costs a bomb. Great big grounds and only an hour and a half from London.

They went into a room looking out onto a terrace. Beyond, dappled lawns, gently shifting trees, black and white cows grazing behind iron railings. Books, leather chairs, a table with magazines – Country Life, The Field, The Economist. "Please, if you would wait here. The Headmaster won't be long."

Alone, they sat, inspected. "I like the atmosphere, don't you, John?"

"Very pleasant, yes." Four hundred a term, near enough. You can tell it's a cut above the Seaford place, though, or the one at St Albans. Bob Wilcox says quite a few City people send their boys here. One or two of the merchant bankers, those kind of people. It's the sort of contact that would do no harm at all. You meet someone, get talking at a cricket match or what have you ... Not at all a bad thing.

"All right, Charles? You didn't get sick in the car, did you?"

The child had black hair, slicked down smooth to his head. His ears, too large, jutted out, transparent in the light from the window, laced with tiny, delicate veins. His clothes had the shine and crease of newness. He looked at the books, the dark brown pictures, his parents, said nothing.

"Come here, let me tidy your hair."

The door opened. The child hesitated, stood up, sat then rose again with his father.

"Mr and Mrs Manders? How very nice to meet you – I'm Margaret Spokes, and will you please forgive my husband who is tied up with some wretch who broke the cricket pavilion window and will be just a few more minutes. We try to be organised but a schoolmaster's day is always just that bit unpredictable. Do please sit down and what will you have to revive you after that beastly drive? You live in Finchley, is that right?"

"Hampstead, really," said the mother. "Sherry would be lovely." She worked over the headmaster's wife from shoes to hairstyle, pricing and assessing. Shoes old but expensive – Russell and Bromley. Good skirt. Blouse could be Marks and Sparks – not sure. Real pearls. Super Victorian ring. She's not gone to any particular trouble – that's just what she'd wear anyway. You can be confident, with a voice like that, of course. Sally Wilcox says she knows all sorts of people.

The headmaster's wife said, "I don't know how much you know about us. Prospectuses don't tell you a thing, do they? We'll look round everything in a minute, when you've had a chat with my husband. I gather you're friends of the Wilcoxes, by the way. I'm awfully fond of Simon – he's down for Winchester, of course, but I expect you know that."

The mother smiled over her sherry. Oh, I know that all right. Sally Wilcox doesn't let you forget that.

"And this is Charles? My dear, we've been forgetting all about you! In a minute I'm going to borrow Charles and take him off to meet some of the boys because after all you're choosing a school for him, aren't you, and not for you, so he ought to know what he might be letting himself in for and it shows we've got nothing to hide."

The parents laughed. The father, sherry warming his guts, thought that this was an amusing woman. Not attractive, of course, a bit homespun, but impressive all the same. Partly the voice, of course; it takes a bloody expensive education to produce a voice like that. And other things, of course. Background and all that stuff.

"I think I can hear the thud of the Fourth Form coming in from games, which means my husband is on they way, and then I shall leave you with him while I take Charles off to the common-room."

For a moment the three adults centred on the child, looking, judging. The mother said, "He looks so hideously pale, compared to those boys we saw outside."

"My dear, that's London, isn't it? You just have to get them out, to get some colour into them. Ah, here's James. James – Mr and Mrs Manders. You remember, Bob Wilcox was mentioning at Sports Day …"

The headmaster reflected his wife's style, like paired cards in Happy Families. His clothes were mature rather than old, his skin well-scrubbed, his shoes clean, his geniality untainted by the least condescension. He was genuinely sorry to have kept them waiting, but in this business one lurches from one minor crisis to the next … And this is Charles? Hello, there, Charles. His large hand rested for a moment on the child's head, quite extinguishing the thin, dark hair. It was as though he had but to clench his fingers to crush the skull. But he took his hand away and moved the parents to the window, to observe the mutilated cricket pavilion, with indulgent laughter.

And the child is borne away by the headmaster's wife. She never touches him or tells him to come, but simply bears him away like some relentless tide, down corridors and through swinging glass doors, towing him like a frail craft, not bothering to look back to see if he is following, confident in the strength of magnetism, or obedience.

And delivers him to a room where boys are scattered among inky tables and rungless chairs and sprawled on a mangy carpet. There is a scampering, and a rising, and a silence falling, as she opens the door.

"Now this is the Lower Third, Charles, who you'd be with if you come to us in September. Boys, this is Charles Manders, and I want you to tell him all about things and answer any questions he wants to ask. You can believe about half of what they say, Charles, and they will tell you the most fearful lies about the food, which is excellent."

The boys laugh and groan; amiable, exaggerated groans. They must like the headmaster's wife: there is licensed repartee. They look at her with bright eyes in open, eager faces. Someone leaps to hold the door for her, and close it behind her. She is gone.

The child stands in the centre of the room, and it draws in around him. The circle of children contracts, faces are only a yard or so from him; strange faces, looking, assessing.

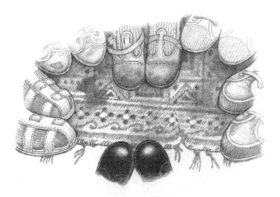

Asking questions. They help themselves to his name, his age, his school. Over their heads he sees beyond the window an inaccessible world of shivering trees and high racing clouds and his voice which has floated like a feather in the dusty schoolroom air dies altogether and he becomes mute, and he stands in the middle of them with shoulders humped, staring down at feet: grubby plimsolls and kicked brown sandals. There is a noise in his ears like rushing water, a torrential din out of which voices boom, blotting each other out so that he cannot always hear the words. Do you? they say, and Have you? and What's your? and the faces, if he looks up, swing into one another in kaleidoscopic patterns and the floor under his feet is unsteady, lifting and falling.

And out of the noises comes one voice that is complete, that he can hear. "Next term, we'll mash you," it says. "We always mash new boys."

And a bell goes, somewhere beyond doors and down corridors, and suddenly the children are all gone, clattering away and leaving him there with the heaving floor and the walls that shift and swing, and the headmaster's wife comes back and tows him away, and he is with his parents again, and they are getting into the car, and the high hedges skim past the car windows once more, in the other directions, and the gravel under the tyres changes to black tarmac.

"Well?"

"I liked it, didn't you?" The mother adjusted the car around her, closing windows, shrugging into her seat.

"Very pleasant, really. Nice chap."

"I liked him. Not quite so sure about her."

"It's pricey, of course."

"All the same …"

"Money well spent, though. One way and another."

"Shall we settle it, then?"

"I think so. I'll drop him a line."

The mother pitched her voice a notch higher to speak to the child in the back of the car. "Would you like to go there, Charles? Like Simon Wilcox? Did you see that lovely gym, and the swimming-pool? And did the other boys tell you all about it?"

The child does not answer. He looks straight ahead of him, at the road coiling beneath the bonnet of the car. His face is haggard with anticipation.

Lullaby

Written by Wendy Cope
Illustration by Raymond Briggs

On a spinning planet
In a starry sky.
There's a little person,
Apple of my eye.

Spin on, spinning planet.
Shine on, starry sky.
Sleep well, little person,
While the night goes by.

Sidecar

From *Puffin Post* by Geraldine McCaughrean
Illustration by Tony Ross

My parents and I parted company at an early age, on account of the sidecar. They were keen bikers – Dad up front, Mum behind – and probably not intending to have a child. But somehow I happened – like a puncture, I suppose. It must have been a blow. The only solution was a sidecar. Dad bolted one on to the DKW.

What places did I visit? What roadside cafes, what scenic viewpoints, what campsites and towns? Sometimes I look at the map and wonder. Even before my eyes changed to brown from milky blue, I was speeding through the Welsh countryside rocked by pot holes and soothed by the sound of a two-stroke engine. It comes back to me in the smell of exhaust fumes.

Welsh roads are fine to bike (if you have enough power and clean spark-plugs). At the top of every hill is a view or a tourist centre. At the bottom of every thrilling downhill career is a racing stream or a chapel. Not that I recall these things from my days in the sidecar. Lying on my back, I could see only the sky. Even sitting up, my head would not have reached the perspex bubble over a Triumph Chariot. No. I have been back. Many times.

In the bottom of a valley on the B5012, a hump-back bridge crosses a stream then turns sharp right. I deduce that the DKW hit the bridge, rose into the air – a thrilling feeling, but bad for the suspension – and the link-pins connecting sidecar to bike simply came out of their holes. On the bend, Dad and Mum went right, but I carried on – through a gate, over a cattle grid, across a field, past a dead tractor, until I met a sheep.

Sheep are solid but well cushioned. And friendly. If it had been a pigsty, I suppose the pigs would have eaten me. As it was, the sheep who adopted me were vegetarians by day and warm by night: a happy combination. We were a close-knit family. Luckily for this story, they were not Welsh speakers, but Bluefaced Leicesters: a noble breed, ultra-proud of their pedigree. What a poor specimen I must have seemed, with no wool, even on my head. I shall never make a decent bedside rug. But if I was a disappointment to them, they never showed it. That is the kind of parents they were.

Luckily they not only spoke but read English, and appreciated
the single word blazoned in gold on my sidecar-cradle: Triumph.
A handsome, promising name, don't you think? They did.

Still, petrol fumes were in my blood. As time passed, I wanted always
to be on the move. As soon as my feet were long enough to cross the
cattle grid in safety, I began my travelling life. In knitted clothes made
by my close-knit family, and in sheepskin boots made from Ancient
Aunt Baabra (she had a good innings), I set off in search of pastures
new. I found Bangor.

Bangor, bangers-and-mash, Bangra music, bang-bang chicken,
Bangkok: all these words fall sweet on my ear. I was fated to work
with cars and bikes, turning old bangers into vintage vehicles. Indeed,
Triumph Sidecar Restorations is known the length and breadth of
Wales. My ambition was to compete in the All Valleys Bike-and-Sidecar
Hill Climb Championships, but a rider needs a partner for that, and
I knew no one with the right qualifications.

I had decided my father was a fool. After all, he had made a hash of
bolting a sidecar to a DKW. My mother was a different matter. In my
imagination, she burned brighter. The sun gleamed on her Cromwell
crash helmet, and her leathers bore a Ferrari prancing horse. I loved her
as only a boy can who has never known his mother. I began to look for
her on the streets of Bangor.

I was sure she must have parted company from my father. Given my
history, it seemed the natural order of things. Spurning his DKW, she
might have cast her eyes towards grander bikes – a Brough Superior
perhaps, or some fancy American Harley with lots of chrome. Even
a car!

So I developed a habit of jumping on the running boards of passing
cars and peering in at any female passengers. I realise this may have
alarmed a few: a boy in a knitted suit, nose flattened against the glass.
Sometimes the driver accelerated to get rid of me, but that was foolish.
No one jumps off a fast-moving car. It isn't sensible.

Anyway, that's how I developed a taste for stunt riding.

With an acetylene torch, one bike and fifteen Royal Enfield Constellation sidecars, I constructed the ultimate stunt. Spreading out from my rear pillion like a peacock's tail rolled a V-formation of conjoined sidecars. There was no shortage of volunteers to man them ... but anyone old enough to sign the insurance waiver weighed too much. The whole shebang sank to its axles. The family rallied round though, and the spectacle of sheep in sidecars seemed to please.

At the critical moment, at the pull of a lever, the sidecars all detached and, like the Red Arrows, spread out in perfect formation. It was short, but well received by Welsh crowds – even better in England where sheep are more of a novelty.

In Oswestry, a women in the crowd became so over-excited that she ran out on to the display ground and was narrowly missed by Uncle Daisy's Constellation. At first my instinct was to let the stewards sort her out. (I'm not good with people: they have neither sparkplugs nor wool.) But on the return run, I saw she was in the grips of a wild grief, rending at her tartan beret.

"Oh woe!" she wailed. "I lost a child in that exact same way. My Morgan! My dearest darling baby Morgan! Lost and gone for ever – the sidecar, too!"

For a moment my heart rose within me – a fleeting, bleating happy thought. But her child had been called Morgan ... If only she had said 'Triumph'! And there was I thinking mine was a fluke tragedy! Perhaps such accidents befall babies every week.

I did not mention to Mrs Jones my own childhood experience, not wanting to set her off again. But I did mention her bottom.

You see Mrs Jones had a perfect bottom. A perfectly massive bottom. In the noble sport of Hill Climbing, you need skill, courage, a perfectly tuned machine ... but most of all you need a big, bulky woman bouncing up and down in the sidecar. It gives the wheels traction – grip. The tyres bite, the bike climbs ...

In teeming rain, Triumph Sidecar and Mrs Jones took the trophy at the 2009 All-Valleys Bike-and Sidecar Hill Climb Championships

(500cc category), climbing 300ft of churned, oozing, trickling mud in just four minutes twenty. Magnificent!

Even watching from the sidelines, my family went home that day muddy to the ears. But (though I blush to say it) they were the proudest sheep in Wales. We make a fine team, Mrs Jones and I.

Doing Things For Myself

Written by Hiawyn Oram
Illustrations by Satoshi Kitamura

They come to do my buttons up
I say, No, Not Today,
Today I'm doing buttons up
My own way.

They come to do my braces up
I say, No, Not Today,
Today I'm doing braces up
My own way.

I like to do things for myself
I wish they'd understand
Only if I ask them to
Should they give me a hand.

I like to do my buttons up
Though never every one
I like to do my buttons up
By leaving some undone.

I like to do my braces up
I like them to be crossed
Without them tied so tightly
My arms might feel all lost.

I like to get my mittens down
By falling from the shelf
I like to wash my face and hands
And miss some dirt, myself.

I like to wet the tablecloth
While filling up my cup
I want the eggs to fly around
While cutting toast squares up.

So that's why I've decided
If they button me today
I'll have to just UNBUTTON things …
My own way.

SNOW

Written by Hiawyn Oram
Illustration by Satoshi Kitamura

Ben likes snow when it's first fallen
And there are only birds' feet in it.
Em likes snow when it's deep
And she falls in it
And it fills her boots.
I like snow when it's icy
And you can slide in it
And toboggan and ride in it.
But when it melts to slush
And it's just wet
We all forget
Just how much we liked it
when
it
was
snow.

That Wrong Thing

Written by Hiawyn Oram
Illustration by Satoshi Kitamura

Sometimes it sits on my shoulders
And sometimes it sits on my head
Sometimes it hides in the curtains
And once it climbed on to my bed.

It isn't exactly a Wob or a Gong
It hasn't a Wob or Gong's face
Though it sneers and it slurks
And it lopples like them
As it follows me round the place.

It isn't exactly a Grissel or Mawk
It hasn't exactly their shape
So I don't bother using my Grissel-Mawk trap
As I know it would only escape.

It isn't exactly a Snaffle or Squirk
Though its shadow can block out the sun
And it snatches, like Snaffles, the light bulbs
And gobbles them one by one.

It isn't exactly a Thing at all
Which is why this is taking so long
It's more like a ... well ...
Like an Urgh-that-Umms-By
WHEN I KNOW I'VE DONE
SOMETHING WRONG!

The Worst Cough in the World

Written by Michael Rosen
Illustration by Mike Brownlow

P oor Elsie! She had the worst cough in the world. It went: cough, cough, cough, cough, cough. Then it stopped for just long enough for her to breathe in: gasp! And then it started again: cough, cough, cough, cough, cough. Nothing seemed to help. Her Mum gave her some medicine. What happened? Cough, cough, cough, cough, cough. Her Mum smeared some greasy stuff on her chest. What happened? Cough, cough, cough, cough, cough. Her Mum gave her a cold drink, a hot drink, a sweet drink, a sour drink. What happened? Well, you know what happened.

Poor Elsie!

Sometimes she cried about it. This meant that she was crying and coughing at the same time.

Mum spoke to the Doctor on the phone and the Doctor said that Mum was doing all the right things. There really wasn't anything else that could be done. Elsie would just have to wait for the cough to go.

There were times when the cough stopped. For a bit, anyway.

Elsie asked Mum, "If the Doctor says that the cough will go, where will it go?"

"Well," said Mum, "it doesn't actually go anywhere, but we could pretend it does, couldn't we? Where would you like it to go?"

"I would like it to go to the pond in the park. It could jump in and disappear underwater."

"Hmm," said Mum, thinking about it, "and I suppose as it went into the water, it would make bubbles: bloop, bloop, bloop."

Elsie laughed.

But then she started coughing again.

And that was nothing to laugh about.

Soon it was bed-time and Mum plumped up the pillows. She said that it would help if Elsie didn't lie flat. She had some more medicine, had some more greasy stuff on her chest, had another drink.

"And shall I leave the window a little, tiny bit open, so that if the cough wants to get out, it can get out through the little crack?" And she winked.

"Yes," said Elsie, "good idea. And it can fly away to the pond."

And so Mum left the window open, just a little, tiny bit, and kissed Elsie goodnight.

Elsie looked round the room, turned over, turned back. She coughed. She turned over.

Suddenly, there was a scurrying noise by the window. It sounded like a small animal trying to get in. But it wasn't making animal noises. It was making what sounded like human tutting noises, just like people make when they're a bit cross. Tut, tut, tut. Then it said, "Really, this isn't very wide. How am I supposed to get in here?"

Elsie sat up on her elbow.

And there she was, a teeny, tiny woman, struggling to get through the crack in the window. She had got most of herself through but she was now trying to pull a bag that was nearly as big herself behind her.

"Really. What do people think? I really wonder." Tut, tut, tut.

Elsie looked at her. She was about the size of her hand and she was wearing an old coat, her hair looked as if it had been blown this way and that in the wind, and she had big rubber boots on.

"Who are you?" Elsie asked.

The teeny, tiny woman didn't answer Elsie's question.

Instead, she said, "It's you is it? Are you the one with the cough?"

"Yes," said Elsie. "But who are you? What are you doing in my bedroom?"

This made the teeny, tiny lady even crosser.

"I was sent for, wasn't I? It was your mother, I guess. She said I had to come tonight and collect. She sounded worried. I said I was too busy. I've got a boy over in Wandsworth, a pair of twins in Hammersmith; I've given a job I was asked to do in Watford to my cousin. I'm not up to going there tonight."

"But … what do you do?"

"Do? Do?" said the teeny, tiny woman. "I'm the Cough Collector," she said.

"Now, I haven't got time to hang about chatting. All I need is a couple of good throaty coughs from you."

"Then what?" Elsie said. "What are you going to do with them?"

"Questions, questions, questions. I collect them in this bag here. Stuff'em in. Then off I fly to the Cough Dump. Offload the two throaty coughs. Then what happens, is that they sit there calling out for their little brothers and sisters. And it draws all the rest of the coughs that you've got inside you, out of the window and off to the dump. Right, no more time for chat. Let's have a bit of coughing from you."

Elsie was stunned. She had never heard of such a thing. And how kind of Mum to arrange this. For a moment, the surprise at what was happening had stopped her coughing. Oh no, she thought, here's my big chance to make the cough go and I haven't got a cough to give to the Cough Collector.

But that didn't last long. A few seconds later, Elsie was off again: cough, cough, cough, cough, cough. Gasp! Cough, cough, cough, cough, cough.

"Whoa, whoah," shouted the teeny, tiny woman. "I only need two." And Elsie could see her stuffing something into her bag.

"Hmm," she said, "that one's a bit green. I don't like them. No worries. We'll have these off to the Dump in a flash. Can't stop. If you can't get back to sleep, young lady, turn yourself inside out. Bye!"

And Elsie watched the Cough Collector climb back out through the window, heaving the bag behind her.

I wonder what she meant about turning myself inside out, she thought. But then she did imagine herself turning inside out, like a jumper and next thing she knew her Mum was standing next to her and it was morning.

"How are you, Poppet?" said Mum.

"I think, I'm OK," Elsie said, not quite sure.

"How's that cough? Did it go off to the pond?"

"No," said Elsie. "The Cough Collector came. She said that you had sent for her. She's taken a couple of throaty coughs off to the Cough Dump and they should pull the rest out too. So long as we leave the window open."

Mum laughed.

"Oh that's very good," she said. "Elsie, that's wonderful."

"No, Mum, you are. I think it's worked. I'm not coughing."

"Yes, of course." Mum said.

"And the Cough Collector's wonderful too," said Elsie.

"Yes," Mum said, "she is."

"How did you get to know her?" asked Elsie.

"Well," said Mum, "erm ... I'm not really sure. I'll have to think about that. In the meantime, you get up and we'll have some breakfast. Toast?"

"Mmm, with jam on, please." said Elsie, still wondering where Mum could have met the Cough Collector.

Call Me Blessed

Written by Jacqueline Wilson
Illustration by Ellen Beier

W hen will it be over? I had no idea it would hurt so much. I want Mother, I want Elizabeth, I want my womenfolk. I had it all planned. It was going to be so beautiful. I was going to stay calm and in control. I wasn't going to cry. I'd lie on my soft bedding in my clean little house and look at the sky through the slit of the window. I'd look up to my Lord and I'd pray to him through every pain.

I try to pray now but the pain keeps flashing through me like lightning and I can't think properly. My whispers become gasps, cries, screams. I call to the Lord because I am his chosen maiden but I can't find him. It's dark and there's just the thunder of my cries and the lightning of my pain.

I don't know what to do. I'm so scared. I didn't ever listen to the other girls when they whispered and giggled about babies. I hated that sort of sniggering. I'd walk away by myself. I'd sing to myself and dance for myself and whisper magical stories to myself. Sometimes the others would follow and make fun of me. I've never fitted in with the other villagers. I haven't any true friends, only my family. Oh Mother, I want you so. And my dear Elizabeth. How did you manage to bear this pain? Your body is becoming frail. I am young and supple and yet I can't stand it.

Oh why couldn't you wait till I was back home in my house, on my soft cushions, with my womenfolk to hold my hands and sponge my face and stroke my poor swollen body. Everything is ready for you at home. There is the little cradle of twigs, the clean linen, the sweet-smelling ointments. Why are you so impatient? Why choose this filthy cave at the back of a stranger's house? The only bed is the straw, the only linen the veil from my head. Why do you want to be born in this dark and lonely place reeking of animal dung?

The cattle munch and murmur, oblivious, but my own little ass lifts its head and brays uneasily as if it's in pain too. It's lame after the long journey. Oh, that endless trek through Samaria, the sharp bones of the little ass chafing my thighs, the dust coating my skin, lining my garments, the tension turning every muscle into sharp stone. I got

so unbearably stiff that I slid down from the ass and tried to walk but I couldn't cope with the clumsiness of my body. I wanted to run like the wind but I could only shamble like a beggar. I had to be helped back onto the little ass, weak and sweating, the pains already flickering in my stomach and spine.

I didn't dare acknowledge them. I stayed silent all that last dusty day. I bent my head so that the pain wouldn't show on my face. I knew it was too soon, I knew I'd have no-one to help me. I knew it was a nightmare when I so wanted it to be like a golden dream. Like my golden dream of Gabriel. The golden voice, the golden heat, the brush of golden wings, and then the golden trumpets inside my head proclaiming my awesome gift from God. I heard the glory of those golden trumpets throughout these last long months. They blared out triumphantly, so that I need not listen to the whispers, the comments, the jeers. They laughed in the village some said I was mad, that I'd always talked to myself and that was a certain sign. Some said I was bad, that I'd lain with other men and should now be tested with the bitter waters. And Joseph said …

Sometimes the trumpets were not quite loud enough. I could hear Joseph's words, I could see his anguish and shame. Some said he should spurn me, some said he should stone me. But he stood up with me in front of all the villagers and he married me, even though he knew I was carrying a child that wasn't his.

"A golden child. God's only son. He chose me, Joseph. An angel came down from Heaven and seared me with the golden spirit and now I have God's golden child within me." I whispered on our wedding night, going down on my knees to Joseph to make him understand. But he couldn't hear the trumpets even though my head rang with their golden harmonies. He turned away from me. He did not lie with me even on our wedding night. He has barely touched me since. His face looks as if it's carved from a rock. But his eyes watch me. They follow me all the time. They are red with anger and grief, although he never lets me see the tears spill. I want to ease his pain but he will not let me be close to him. He is a rock man, hard and unyielding. He has left me now, in my lonely agony. He is out walking in the dark while I writhe here in the straw.

"Joseph, for pity's sake, come to me!"

I call again and again. I call until my voice is hoarse. And then I hear a rustle in the straw, sense a larger shape above me, smell the faint scent of sycamore clinging to his clothing. He crouches beside me. There's a lull between the lightning and I struggle to sit up, to see his face in the murk of the moonlight. I see that salt glitter on his cheeks.

"Don't hate me, husband," I gasp.

"I don't hate you, Mary. I've tried to hate you but I love you too much. I've loved you since you were a small girl skipping past my shop. Remember, I pinned a few wood-shavings in your hair for fancy curls. You looked so shy and solemn at first but then you saw your shadow in the sunlight and you smiled at your silly curls. That smile stirred strong feelings in my heart. I knew then that all I wanted in the whole world was to make you my wife. I am your husband now but I am helpless. I don't know what to do for you. I can't bear to see you struggling like this."

"Stay with me. Please stay with me."

The lightning strikes and I scream and flail my arms and he catches hold of me, gripping with his strong hands until the flashing is finished.

"I'll stay with you," Joseph whispers into the darkness. "You are my wife and I am your husband. I will stay."

I have lived as a maiden since my marriage but now the storm in my body blows away all my modesty. I forget I'm me, Mary. I am part of the storm, the bellow of thunder, the flash of lightning, and I rage. I am torn one way, torn another, torn until I am suddenly, shockingly split into two. Two people. I am one and you are the other. Still joined but separate. The storm is over.

I reach down and hold you in my hands. I stare at you in wonder. I stare at the bloom of your cheeks, pink as pomegranates. I stare at the milky paleness of your tiny wrists, the spider web delicacy of your veins. I lay you on my head-dress but before I swaddle you I want to worship you. I rub my cheek against the damp tendrils of your hair. I kiss one tiny curled foot. I touch one small clenching fist and it fastens round my finger. There is no doubt now. You are my golden gift from God.

I wrap you up reverently, my hands trembling. I hold you in my arms and shudder as one more lightning flicker contracts my womb. In that searing second I see myself still holding you in my arms when you're a grown man. A golden grown man and yet you seem as stiff and still as a babe in swaddling clothes. Tears stream from my eyes although I don't understand.

"Don't cry, my sweet little wife," Joseph whispers, and he kisses my eyes. "The pain is all over now."

But I know it is only just beginning.

Kanai the Gardener

From *The Ocean of Story* by Caro Ness
Illustration by Jacqui Mair

Kanai, the Rajah's gardener, had the greenest fingers in the kingdom. He talked as he worked, and the plants seemed to thrive on his voice and touch. Trees, shrubs, and flowers had been brought from every corner of the globe, and each one, tended by Kanai, grew to twice its usual size. Frangipani, roses, lotus flowers, lilies; the garden was a bright, fragrant paradise. There was just one puzzle that Kanai had yet to solve: each night the choicest fruits in the garden were eaten by some mysterious creature.

Kanai usually left the garden at dusk, but one night he had more work to do than usual and it was almost midnight before he thought about going home. The earthy smell of evening still hung in the air, but the moon was full, and sharp fingers of light lit the silent garden. Suddenly the peace was broken by a tremendous crash. The earth seemed to shift underfoot and the trees bent and groaned. Terrified, Kanai hid behind a tree.

An enormous elephant came down from the sky and into the garden. After much thought, Kanai realized that this could only be Oirabot, the heavenly elephant, and he was determined to follow it and see where it went and what it did. Kanai shadowed Oirabot as he roamed around the garden, pulling up the tenderest shoots and plucking the ripest fruits from the trees. He couldn't help noticing that despite the elephant's enormous size, the garden was not damaged in any way.

When the elephant had finally eaten its fill and looked as if it was about to leave, Kanai grasped its tail and clung on grimly. Oirabot began to soar upward, oblivious of his passenger.

As soon as they arrived in heaven, Kanai let go of Oirabot's tail. Everything was so huge, much bigger than in the Rajah's garden even! Enormous mangoes, tea plantations like forests, cows as big as elephants, and elephants the size of houses! And everything was so cheap! Kanai bought a mango and betel nut to show his wife, then gorged himself until sunset. Some time later, his stomach tight and his head heavy, he found Oirabot and sat down beside him to wait until he made his journey back to earth.

That night Oirabot returned to the garden for his midnight feast with Kanai clinging onto his tail. As soon as they were on firm ground, Kanai loosened his grip and hurried home to his wife. She was beside herself with worry, since her husband was usually reliable and she had not seen him for two whole days.

"Where on earth have you been? I asked everyone I could think of if they had seen you, but no one had!"

Without saying a word, Kanai handed her the mango and the betel nut. When she saw them, his wife danced around with excitement.

"Where did you get them? Where did you get them?"

Kanai told her all about his adventures and how cheap and plentiful food was in heaven.

"I want to go too! Take me with you tonight!" said his wife.

"All right! All right! But whatever you do, don't tell anyone else about this. It must be our secret."

"I wouldn't dream of telling anyone else," his wife retorted.

Later that afternoon, Kanai's wife went to the well to fetch some water. Her best friend was there.

"It won't hurt to tell my best friend," thought Kanai's wife. So, swearing her to secrecy, she told her friend the whole story.

Well, that friend told her best friend and she in turn told her best friend, who told her husband, who told his brother, and soon everyone in the town had heard the story. They all arrived at Kanai's house demanding to be taken to heaven. What could Kanai do? He had to agree. Everyone flocked to the garden to wait for Oirabot. When the elephant appeared, Kanai said, "This is what we'll do. As Oirabot is about to leave, I'll grab his tail with one hand, then my wife will hold my other hand, her friend will hold onto her, and so on. That way, we'll all get to heaven."

When Oirabot showed signs of leaving, Kanai seized his tail and they all formed a chain, as agreed. The elephant climbed higher and higher. He was almost past the seventieth star when Kanai's wife's best friend asked, "How big was the betel nut your husband brought home?"

Kanai's wife repeated the question to her husband. "Just wait and see!" he replied.

"That's not good enough! She wants to know now!" said Kanai's wife.

Kanai, utterly exasperated, said, "They were about this big." As he spoke, he let go of the elephant's tail and stretched his hands out to show the size, and Kanai, with his wife and all their friends, tumbled head over heels back down to earth.

The Dayspring

Written by Martin Waddell
Illustration by Adrienne Salgado

A stone hero lay in a cathedral, Major Arbuthnot, V.C., surrounded by flags and drums.

In a stall on the wall above Major Arbuthnot, V.C., were John William Lennox and Maud, carved in wood.

All day the cathedral was busy but, at night, when the people had gone, there was peace and quiet.

Then, one night, with a roar and a shake, the world BROKE!

In the mess and the rubble lay John William Lennox and Maud. There was no more of Major Arbuthnot. He'd gone west, with the rest.

"What's all this about then, Johnny?" asked Maud, sitting up.

"Well I'm bothered," said John William Lennox. "You're talking!"

"It's right queer, ain't it?" said Maud. "I thought I was just made of wood!"

"It was good wood," said John William Lennox, "and old!"

"But that doesn't explain you and me talking!" said Maud.

They got up and shook themselves down and looked all about them, at the ruins.

"Is anyone there?" shouted John William Lennox.

"Please help us!" cried Maud.

Nobody came. Nothing stirred. They clung close together in the dirt and the dust, John William Lennox and Maud.

"We're out on our own, lass!" said John William Lennox.

"I don't like it, our Johnny!" said Maud. "What do we think we're about?"

"I haven't a clue, lass," said John William Lennox. "But I think, pretty soon, we'll find out!" They both shouted again, but nobody came.

"Maybe it's Him," said John William Lennox, "happen He's made a mistake, and blowed the lot up!"

"I don't think He'd do that!" said Maud. "It was them and their soldiers and guns!"

"Reckon you're right!" said John William Lennox. "But that isn't much to comfort us.

And then came a GLOW.

"Don't look now, lass!" said John William Lennox. "But there's something up there!"

"What is it?" said Maud.

"I can't rightly tell," said John William Lennox. "But I think it's looking at us!"

And then ... a Voice came.

"You awright, lads?" it asked.

"We're rightly!" said John William Lennox.

"Right poorly!" said Maud, "and just a shade battered to boot!"

"Never mind," said the Voice.

"BUT WE DO!" said John William Lennox and Maud, who were feeling ... well, odd.

"I thought the old place was in a bit of a mess, lads," said the Voice. "So I thought, 'Better chuck it and start again!' So I have, and I did, and you're IT! And good luck, 'cause I reckon you'll need it."

Then the glow faded away. They were left in the dust, feeling dazed.

"Who was that, lass?" whispered John William Lennox.

"It was Him," said Maud, "Him up There, like imagine Him picking on us."

"But why us, lass?" asked John William Lennox.

"Why not us?" said Maud.

"Because we're made of wood!" said John William Lennox. "Though it is good wood, and old!"

"Reckon He trusts us," said Maud. "He's trusting us to trust Him!"

"That's not much of an answer!" said John William Lennox.

"It is all that you're getting!" said Maud.

"Well then we'd better get started," said John William Lennox, "though I don't rightly know how to start!"

"Get digging and planting!" said Maud.

And they did.

They did what they could, the two bits of wood, digging and planting, but it takes a long time making a world without soldiers and guns and cathedrals and flags.

But they did what they could ... John William Lennox and Maud.

You Don't Look Very Poorly

Adapted from *Crummy Mummy And Me* by Anne Fine
Illustration by Rose Fay

Y ou don't exactly ask to get sick, do you? I mean, you don't go around inviting germs and viruses to move in and do their worst to your body. You don't actually apply for trembling legs and feeling shivery, and a head that's had a miniature steel band practising for a carnival in it all night.

And if you should happen to mention to your own mother that you feel absolutely terrible, you would expect a bit of sympathy, wouldn't you?

I wouldn't. Not any more.

"You don't look very poorly."

That's what she said. And she said it suspiciously too, as if I was one of those people who's always making excuses to stay off school and spend the day watching The Teletubbies, Countdown and old black and white films.

"Well, I feel absolutely rotten."

"You don't look it."

"I'm sorry!" I snapped. (I was getting pretty cross.) "Sorry I can't manage a bright-green face for you! Or purple spots on my belly! Or all my hair falling out! But I feel rotten just the same!"

And I burst into tears.

(Now that is not like me.)

"Now that's not like you," said Mum, sounding sympathetic at last, "You must be a little bit off today."

"I am not off," I snarled through my tears. "I'm not left-over milk. Or rotten fish."

"There, there," Mum soothed. "Don't fret, Minna. Don't get upset. You just hop straight back up those stairs like a good poppet, and in a minute I'll bring you up something nice on a tray, and you can have a quiet day in bed, with Mum looking after you until you feel better."

That was a bit more like it, as I think you'll agree. So I stopped snivelling and went back to bed. I didn't exactly hop straight back up those stairs because I was feeling so crummy and weak I could barely drag myself up hanging on to the banisters; but I got up somehow, and put on my dressing gown and buttoned it right to the top to keep my chest warm, and plumped up my pillows so I could sit comfortably, and switched on my little plastic frog reading-lamp and folded my hands in my lap, and I waited.

And I waited.

And I waited.

(In case you are wondering, I was waiting for Mum to bring me up something nice on a tray and look after me until I felt better.)

She never came.

Oh, I'm sure that she meant to come. I'm sure she had every intention of coming. I'm sure it wasn't her fault the milkman came and needed paying, and it took time to work out what she owed because he'd been away for two weeks on his holiday in Torremolinos.

And I'm sure it wasn't Mum's fault that he took the opportunity to park his crate of bottles down on the doorstep and tell her all about the way some sneaky people always bagged the best pool-loungers by creeping down at dead of night and dropping their swimming towels over them; and how his wife's knees burned and peeled but none of the rest of her; and how his daughter Meryl came home to her job at the Halifax with a broken heart because of some fellow called Miguel Angel Alvarez Lopez de Mantana, who danced like a fury but turned out to be engaged to a Spanish girl working in Barcelona.

Oh, it wasn't Mum's fault that she had to listen to all that before she could get away to bring me up something on a tray and look after me until I was better. But I could hear them talking clearly enough on the doorstep. And I don't actually recall hearing her say firmly but politely: 'Excuse me, Mr Hooper, but Minna's in bed feeling terrible, and I must get back upstairs, so I'll listen to all the rest tomorrow.' I heard quite a bit; but I didn't hear that.

As soon as the milkman had chinked off next door, I thought I heard Mum making for the bottom of the stairs. But she never got there.

"YeeeeoooooowwwwwwwaaaaaAAAAAAAAAAA-EEEEWWW!"

You guessed it. My baby sister woke up.

Rose Fay

And I suppose it wasn't Mum's fault that Miranda needed her nappy changing. And that there weren't any dry ones because we don't have a tumble-drier and it had been raining for three solid days. And Mum had forgotten to pick up another packet of disposables last time she practically swam down to the shops.

So Mum decided the simplest thing would be to park Miranda in the playpen where little accidents don't matter. It wasn't her fault it took forever to drag it out of the cupboard because she had dumped my sledge, and the dress-up box, and all the empty jars she's saving for Gran right in front of it. Or that she had to fetch the damp nappies off the line and drape them over the rack in the kitchen.

And I suppose it's understandable that while she was shaking out the damp nappies, she should glance out of the window at the grey skies and think about nipping down to the launderette with the rest of the washing and handing it to Mrs Hajee to do in the washing machines, since it didn't look as if it would ever stop raining.

So I suppose it does make sense that the very next thing I heard on my quiet day in bed was Mum bellowing up the stairs: "Minna! Minna! Look after the baby for a few minutes will you, while I nip down to the launderette? She's perfectly happy in her playpen with her toys. Just come down if she starts to squawk."

Fine. Lovely. Sure. Here am I, feeling terrible and looking forward to something nice on a tray and being looked after until I feel better, and suddenly, I'm looking after the baby!! Fine. Lovely. Sure.

To be quite fair to Mum, she didn't stay out any longer than was absolutely necessary. There was the launderette of course. And then she had to get disposable nappies or Miranda would have had to spend the whole morning sitting on her cold bottom in the playpen, waiting for the ones in the kitchen to dry. And whilst she was in the supermarket she did pick up bread, and a quarter of sliced ham, and a few oranges and a couple of other things, making too many to get through the quick checkout. And there were really long queues at the others because it was pension-day morning. And she did just pop into the newsagent's on her way home as well. And, yes, she did stop on the corner for a second, but that was just to be polite to the Lollipop Lady who told her that, whatever it was I'd got, there was a lot of it about, and mum ought to be really careful or she'd come down with it as well.

And then she came straight home. She says she was out for no more than five minutes at the very most. But I've a watch, so I know better.

Then, at last, she came up to my room. She had Miranda tucked under one arm, all bare bottom and wriggles, and she was carrying a tray really high in the air, practically above her head, so my sister couldn't upset it with all her flailing arms and legs. It was so high I couldn't see what was on it from the bed.

"I don't know how these nurses do it," said Mum. "They should have medals pinned on their chests, not watches."

I looked at mine. It was exactly 10.30. (I fell sick at 8.23.)

"If you were a nurse," I said, "you would have got the sack two hours ago."

"I'd like to see you do any better," she snapped back, sharpish.

"I bet I would," I told her. "I bet if you were sick, it wouldn't take me two whole hours to bring you something nice on a tray."

"I should wait till you see what there is on the tray before you start grumbling," Mum warned. And then she lowered it on to the bed in front of me.

And there was a cup of very milky coffee with bubbles on top in my favourite fat china bear mug, and a huge orange cut into the thinnest possible circular slices just how I like it when I want to nibble at the peel as well. And a chocolate biscuit bar and the latest Beano and Go Girl!, and a pack of twenty brand-new fine-tipped-pens.

I felt dead guilty for being so grumpy. "I'm sorry I said you'd get the sack as a nurse."

"Is that true?"

"Certainly."

And then, with my baby sister safe at last, mum sat down on my bed and took a break.

I thought about what she said quite a lot while I was getting better. As I sipped my coffee, and nibbled my orange circles, and read my Beano, and made my chocolate biscuit last as long as I could while I was drawing with my brand-new felt pens, I wondered what sort of patient Mum would make. She isn't famous in this house for long-suffering meekness or sunny patience.

And I wondered what sort of nurse I'd make – sensitive, deft, unflappable, efficient …

I'd no idea I would find out so soon.

It was only two days later, on Saturday morning, that Mum leaned over the banisters and called down: "Minna, I feel just awful. Awful."

"You don't look very poorly."

(I didn't mean it that way. It just popped out.)

You'd have thought she was trying to suggest she was faking.

"I may not look it but I am," she snapped. "I feel as if I've been left out all night in the rain, and my bones have gone soggy, and hundreds of spiteful little men with steel boots are holding a stamping competition in my brain."

Personally, even without the Lollipop Lady saying there was a lot of it about, I would have recognised the symptoms at once.

I was determined to show Mum what proper nursing ought to be.

"You go straight back to bed," I ordered. "I'll take care of you, and everything else. You tuck yourself in comfortably, and I'll bring up something nice on a tray."

Mum swayed a little against the banisters. She did look pale.

"You are an angel, Minna," she said faintly. And wrapping her shiny black skull-and-crossbones dressing-gown more closely around her string-vest nightie, she staggered back into the bedroom.

I don't have to tell you about my plan, do I? You'll already have guessed. Yes, I was going to rush back into the kitchen and spread a tray with lovely, tempting treats for an invalid's breakfast – treats like a cup of tea made just the way Mum really likes it, golden-pale, not that lovely, thick, murky, dark sludge favoured by me and Gran. (We joke

that Mum's tea is too weak to crawl out of the pot.) And I was going
to pick a tiny posy of flowers from the garden, and arrange them in one
of the pretty china egg cups.

And I was going to bring the tray up without delay.

Guess what went wrong first. No, don't bother. I'll tell you. First,
I locked myself out. Honest. Me. Minna. The only one in the house
who never does it. I did it. I was so keen to get my tray arranged that
I stepped out of the back door into the garden to find flowers without
checking the latch.

Clunk!

The moment I heard the door close behind me, I realized. I could
have kicked myself in the shins. I picked my way around to the front
door, just on the off-chance that the front door was unlocked. But I
knew it wouldn't be, and of course it wasn't.

I stood there, thinking. I had two choices. I could ring the doorbell
and drag poor, shaking, deathly pale Mum from her bed of sickness
and down the stairs to let me in; or I could slip next door to old Mrs
Pitopoulos, ring her bell instead, and ask to borrow the spare key to our
house she keeps for emergencies in an old cocoa tin under her sink.

I knew which a good nurse would do. I went next door and rang the bell.

No answer.

I rang again.

Still no answer.

Suddenly I noticed a faint scrabbling overhead. I looked up, and
there was Mrs Pitopoulos in her quilted dressing-gown, fighting the stiff
window-catch with her arthritic fingers. She couldn't budge it, so she
just beckoned me inside the house.

I tried the front door. It was locked. I went round the back, and that
door opened. I picked my way through the furry sea of all her pet cats
rubbing their arched backs against my legs, so pleased to see me, and
went upstairs.

Mrs Pitopoulos was sitting on the edge of her bed. Her face looked
like a wrinkled sack, and her wig was all crooked.

"You look very poorly," I told her.

I couldn't help it. It just popped out.

"Oh Minna," she said. "I feel terrible, terrible. My legs are rubber, and there are red hot nails in my head."

"I've had that," I said. "Mum's got it now. The Lollipop Lady says that there's a lot of it about."

When she heard this, Mrs Pitopoulos began to look distinctly better. Maybe when you're that age and you get sick, you think whatever it is has come to get you. At any rate, she tugged her wig round on her head, and even the wrinkles flattened out a bit.

"Minna," she said, "Would you do me a great favour, and feed my hungry cats?"

"What about you?" I said. "Have you had anything this morning?"

"Oh, I'm not hungry," Mrs Pitopoulos declared.

But then she cocked her head on one side, and wondered about it. And then she added, "Maybe I do feel just a little bit peckish. Yesterday my sister brought me all these lovely things: new-laid brown speckled eggs and home-made bread and a tiny pot of fresh strawberry jam. But what I'd really like is …" (Her eyes were gleaming, and she looked miles better.) "What I'd really like is a bowl of Heinz tomato soup with bits of white bread floating on the top."

Even I can cook that …

And so I did. And fed her cats. And she was so pleased when I brought the soup up to her on a tray that she pressed on me all the little gifts her sister had brought around the day before: the new-laid brown speckled eggs and home-made bread and tiny pot of strawberry jam – oh, and the door key of course.

Mum was astonished when I brought the tray up. I thought she must have been asleep. She looked as if she had been dozing. She heaved herself upright against the pillows, and I laid the tray down on her knees.

"Minna!" she cried. "Oh how lovely! Look at the flowers!"

"Wait till you've tasted the food," I said.

I could tell she didn't really feel much like eating. But she was determined not to hurt my feelings, so she reached out and took one of the strips of hot buttered toast made from the home-made bread.

She nibbled the crust politely.

"Delicious," she said. And then, "Mmmm. Delicious."

She couldn't help dipping the next strip of toast into the new-laid brown speckled soft-boiled egg.

"Mmmm!" she cried. "This is wonderful."

After the egg was eaten, she still had two strips of toast left. She spread one with fresh strawberry jam, and off she went again.

"Mmmm! Marvellous!"

She went into raptures over the golden-pale tea. (I reckoned I'd have a battle ever forcing her back to medium-brown, when she felt well again.) And she leaned back against the pillows smiling. She looked a lot better.

"I'll bring you some more, if you'd like it," I offered.

"You are the very best nurse." Mum declared. "You managed all this, and so quickly too!"

Now I was sure she'd been dozing. I'd taken ages.

"You're the very best patient." I returned the compliment. "You don't notice what's going on or how long it takes!"

"Silly," she said, and snuggled back under the bedclothes.

I think she must have thought I was joking.

Chocs

Written by Carol Ann Duffy
Illustration by Sam Usher

Into the half-pound box of
Moonlight
my small hand crept,
There was an electrifying rustle.
There was a dark and glamorous scent.
Into my open, religious mouth
the first Marzipan Moment went.

Down in the crinkly second layer
five finger-piglets snuffled
among the Hazelnut Whirl,
the Caramel Swirl,
the Black Cherry and Almond Truffle.

Bliss.

I chomped, I gorged,
I stuffed my face,
till only the Coffee Cream
was left for the owner of the box –
tough luck, Ann Pope –
oh, and half an Orange Supreme.

The Best of Times

Written by Michael Morpurgo
Illustrations by Emma Chichester Clark

T here are times when all seems well with the world. It was just such a time when this story begins. Everyone in the whole country was happy. The harvest was looking good. The corn grew gold in the fields. The vines and the trees were heavy with fruit. The shining rivers teemed with silver fish.

But happiest of all in this lucky land was Prince Frederico. He was more like a brother than a prince to his people, and much loved, which was why everyone was so happy for him when he found at last the Princess of his heart, Princess Serafina. She was a girl of such beauty and kindness that everyone who saw her took her to their heart at once. She only had to smile and there was joy all around her. She sang, she danced. She only had to laugh and the world laughed with her.

The two married on New Year's Day, and the people went mad with joy. They rang the bells all over the land. They danced in the street, they rousted and revelled, they feasted and fêted from morning till night. Never had anyone seen such a happy couple.

But a year or so later, all this had changed. The joy and the gladness had gone. Everyone could see that a great sorrow was settling over the Princess, like a dark shadow.

She never smiled any more, nor laughed any more. She did not sing. She did not dance. She did not speak for days on end. Sometimes she would not even eat. Prince Frederico simply could not understand what had come over his beloved Princess, nor could anyone else. It was a complete mystery.

The light left her eyes. The glow left her cheeks. Every evening, the Princess would sit beside her Prince in the great hall of the palace, not touching her food, speaking to no one. She seemed lost in her own sadness, and could find no way out.

Prince Frederico was desperate to make her happy again. He did all he could to cheer her heart.

At Christmas time, as a token of his love for her, he lavished gifts upon her. Dresses of the finest silk. Rubies and emeralds and sapphires he gave her too, and a pair of white doves that cooed to her from her window when she woke in the mornings. He gave her parakeets and peacocks, meercats and monkeys, and two whippets to stay always by her side and love her faithfully.

But nothing seemed to raise her spirits. No husband could have been more kind and loving than the Prince. He tried his very best to find out why it was, how it was, that she had become so wrapped up in her sorrows.

"We can be happy together again, dearest," he told her. "All will be well, I promise. If only you would just tell me what it is that is troubling you so then I could help to make things right for you, and make you happy again. Is it something I have done?"

But the Prince's kind words, like all his wonderful gifts, simply left her cold. She turned her head away and kept her silence. Even when he held her in his arms and kissed her fondly, she still seemed far away from him and lost in her sadness. The Prince was heartbroken. There seemed to be nothing whatever he could do to help her. The royal physician visited her every day but he was as baffled and mystified as everyone else. No medicine he gave her made any difference.

For poor Princess Serafina there was no escape from her sorrows, even in her dreams. All night long she would lie awake. All day long she would sit in her room, ignoring the food Prince Frederico brought to her, however sweet it smelt, however spicy. A little fruit was all she would eat, and a little water to drink. That was all. She was overwhelmed by sorrow. Maybe after the grey skies of winter had passed, the Prince thought, maybe then she would be happier.

Spring came at long last, and there was birdsong again, and daffodils danced in the sunshine. But the Princess remained as sad as ever. Prince Frederico was now becoming worried for her life, as was the royal physician.

"She is pining away, my Prince," the physician told him, his eyes full of tears. "She seems to have lost the will to live. If she does not want to live, then there is little I can do, little anyone can do. All I can suggest is that she should get out into the fresh Spring air. Maybe she should go for a ride each day. That might help."

So the next morning, Prince Frederico took her for a long ride up in the hills, where the air was bright and bracing, where they could look out over the land and see how green and lovely it was under a cloudless blue sky. He put his arm around her.

"Isn't this the most beautiful place on earth, dearest?" he whispered. "It makes you feel good to be alive, doesn't it?"

But Princess Serafina spoke not a word in reply. She gazed out over the cornfields, seeing nothing but emptiness, feeling nothing but loneliness.

By the time spring turned to summer, the Princess had become too weak even to ride. The Prince loved her far too much to give up trying. Day after day, he took her out walking in the countryside. But nothing seemed to mean anything to her any more; not the warmth of the breeze on her face, not the buzzards wheeling and mewing over the hillsides, not the lark rising into the sky from the cornfield, not the leaping salmon, nor the whisper of the willows by the river. Nothing touched her heart.

Now it was Autumn. The Princess was too ill by this time to go out any more for her daily walks with the Prince. Instead he sat with her at her window, holding her hand, hoping and praying for the first sign of a miraculous recovery. None came. Gentle morning mists lay over the water-meadows. Trees glowed red and gold and yellow in the afternoon sun. But the Princess saw no beauty in it, took no joy from it at all.

Winter came in with its whining winds and savage storms. The Prince and Princess sat by the fire now in her room, and he would read her stories through the long dark evenings, even though he could tell she wasn't listening. Then, just a week or so before Christmas it was, the Princess became too weak even to rise from her bed. The royal physician shook his head and told the Prince that he knew of nothing that could save her now, that he must prepare himself for the worst.

"No!" cried the Prince. "She will not die. I will not let her die."
But he feared in his heart of hearts that there was nothing more
that he could do.

Inside the palace, and outside too, the news quickly spread that
the Princess was close to death, that it could only be a matter of time.
The Master of the Prince's Household ordered that all preparations for
Christmas were to be stopped, that the holly was to be removed, the
tree taken down from the great hall, that there would be no Christmas
celebrations that year.

All about him, the Prince saw only sympathy and sadness. Friends
and family wept openly. It was more than he could bear. He just wanted
to get away from it all. He leapt on to his horse and galloped off into
the countryside where he could be alone. He rode and he rode, crying

out his grief, shouting it into the wind, into the blinding blizzard that was suddenly swirling all around him. On he rode through the snowstorm, not knowing any more how far he had gone, nor where he was, not caring much either.

Soon his horse could go no further. The snow was too deep, the wind too harsh. So when the Prince saw the light of a cottager window nearby, he knew he had to stop and seek shelter.

But as he came closer and dismounted from his horse, the Prince realised that it wasn't a cottage at all, but a caravan, a travellers' caravan.

He climbed the steps and knocked on the door.

A smiling young lad opened the door and invited him in at once. He did not appear at all surprised to see him. In fact, it seemed to the Prince that his whole family of travellers must somehow have been expecting him, so generous and immediate, so unquestioning was the warmth of their welcome. They saw to the Prince's horse, stabled her with theirs, made sure she had a good rub-down and a feed. Then they sat the Prince down by the stove and gave him a bowl of piping-hot soup to warm him through. In the glow of the lanterns there were a dozen or more faces watching him as he drank down his soup, old and young, but all of them welcoming. There was no sadness here, only smiles and laughter wherever he looked.

None of them seemed to know who he was. He was simply a stranger they had taken in out of the storm.

All evening he stayed with them as they sang their songs and told their stories. Then the old grandfather, the head of the family, leant forward to speak to the Prince.

"You've heard our songs, stranger, and you've heard our stories. Haven't you got a song you'd like to sing for us? Haven't you got a story you'd like to tell?"

The Prince thought for a while. He had only one story on his mind. "It's about a Prince who lived in a palace, and a beautiful Princess whom he loved more than life itself, how they had once been so happy, until …" And so he told his story.

As he neared the end of his story, one of the children sitting at his feet looked up at him and cried, "And did the Princess die? I don't want her to die."

"Nor do I," said the Prince. 'I want my story to have a happy ending. I so want her to live. But, you see, I don't know how to save her from her sadness, how to make her happy again. All of you here seem to be so happy. What's your secret?"

"Oh, that's quite simple," replied the old grandfather, knocking out his pipe on the stove. "We are who we want to be. We're travellers, and we keep travelling on. We just follow the bend in the road. Like everyone, we have our troubles, we have our sadnesses. But we try to keep smiling. That's the most important thing of all, to keep smiling. Now if that Princess in your story could only smile, then she'd be right as rain, and your story would have a happy ending. I like a happy ending. But there's a strange thing about happy endings, they often make you cry, don't they? Funny that. Very close those two, crying and laughing. We need a bit of both, I reckon." The old grandfather lit up his pipe again before he went on. "This Prince of yours, in the story, he loves his Princess very much doesn't he?"

"More than his whole kingdom," said the Prince. "He'd give his whole kingdom to have her happy again."

"Well then, maybe that's just what he'll have to do," said the old man.

The Prince lay awake all night beside the stove, the travelling family sleeping on the floor around him, and all the while he was thinking of everything the old grandfather had said. Outside, the storm was blowing itself out.

By morning the Prince had made up his mind what must be done to save his beloved Serafina. He ate a hearty breakfast with the family, and thanked all of them for their kindliness from the bottom of his heart. Then, wishing them a happy Christmas, he set spurs to his horse and rode homeward through the snow, hoping and praying all the way that Princess Serafina would be no worse when he got there.

She was no worse, but she was no better either. Prince Frederico knew there was no time to lose. He called his Council together at once.

"Send out messengers into every corner of this land," he told them. "Tell the people that I will give away my whole kingdom, all my titles, lands and property to anyone who is able to make Princess Serafina smile again."

The Council protested loudly at this, but the Prince would hear no argument from them.

"I want it proclaimed that whoever can do this, whoever wishes to win my kingdom, must come here to the palace on Christmas Day – and that is only two days away now." He turned to the Master of the Household. "Meanwhile, we shall make merry throughout the palace, throughout the land, as we always do at Christmas time. I want there to be no more sadness. I want the Princess to feel the joy of Christmas all around her. I want this palace to be loud with laughter. I want to hear the carols ringing out. I want her to smell all the baking pies and puddings, all the roasting pork and geese. I want everything to be just as it should be. We may be sad, but we must make believe we are glad. Let her know that Christmas is the best of times. Let her see it, let her hear it."

And so messengers were sent out far and wide, into every valley, into every hamlet and town in the land.

Meanwhile, as the Prince had commanded, every room and hall in the palace was bedecked again for Christmas, and all the festive fun and games began.

By the first light of dawn on Christmas Day, the courtyard of the palace was filled with all manner of jesters and clowns, jugglers and acrobats and contortionists, all in bright and wonderful costumes, all busy rehearsing their acts. There were animals too – elephants from India, ponies from Spain and chimpanzees from Africa.

Inside the great hall, everyone waited for Prince Frederico to appear and, when at last they saw him coming down the staircase carrying Princess Serafina in his arms, they were on their feet and cheering them to the rafters, willing her to be better, longing for her to smile.

How pale she looked, how frail, so frail that many thought she might not live to see in the New Year. But everyone there that Christmas Day knew that this would be her last chance, the only hope, and that they had their part to play. They would do all they could to lift her spirits, to let her know how much she was loved. When at last the great doors opened and in came the first of the performers, a clown with a bucket on his head, they all roared with laughter, all of them glancing from time to time at the Princess, hoping for a flicker of a smile.

One after the other, the clowns and jesters came in to do their turns. They cavorted and capered, they tripped and tumbled, but through it all the Princess sat stony-faced. Jugglers and acrobats, the best in the land, cartwheeled and somersaulted around the hall. They amazed and enthralled everyone there, but not the Princess. Everyone howled with laughter at the contortionists' tangled tricks, but not the Princess.

When the elephants came trumpeting in, the chuckling chimpanzees riding on their backs, when the ponies danced and pranced in time to the music, the Princess looked on bemused, unamused, and empty-hearted. As the last of them left, and the great doors closed after them, a silence fell upon the hall, a silence filled with sorrow. Prince Frederico knew, as everyone did, that it was hopeless now, that nothing on Earth could lighten the darkness for the Princess, that she was lost to them forever.

But just then, slowly, very slowly, one of the great doors groaned open, and a face peered around. A masked face.

"Who are you?" Prince Frederico asked, as into the hall there came a whole troupe of players. They wore no costumes, only masks. Some were older, some were younger, they could see that. And some were women and some men. But all moved lightly on their feet, like dancers. Together, hands joined, they walked the length of the great hall to where the Prince and Princess sat.

"Who are you?" the Prince asked them once again.

"We are a donkey," said one.

"We are a camel," said another.

"We are a cow."

"We are a sheep."

"We are a goat."

"I am a goose."

"And I am a star," a small voice piped up, holding up high a golden star on a long pole. "And we have all made a puppet play for the Princess, a Christmas play, to please her heart." With that, everyone except the child with the star went out again.

Moments later, a goose appeared at the great door, looking imperiously this way and that, as if the palace belonged to him. And then, bold as brass, as if no one else had any right to be there, he waddled into the great hall, stopping to beckon in after him a sheep and a goat and a cow, life-sized all of them, and all of them – the goose too – manipulated by masked puppeteers. They breathed such life into their puppets that, very soon, everyone had eyes only for the animals themselves, and the puppeteers became almost invisible. Organised by this bossy goose, who was fast becoming a favourite with the audience, the animals settled down to sleep under the golden star.

A donkey walked in then, a weary-looking donkey. On his back he was carrying a lady who wore a dark cloak about her – everyone knew it was Mary by now, of course. And leading the donkey was Joseph, who helped her down off the donkey, and led her in amongst the sleeping animals, where he sat her down to rest. They sang a carol together then: "Silent night, holy night, all is calm, all is bright." As they finished singing, Mary opened up her cloak very slowly, and everyone saw there was a baby inside.

A gasp ran around the hall, as everyone saw that the child too was a puppet. His little fists waved in the air. He kicked his legs. He cried out. He gurgled. Suddenly, the Princess was sitting bolt upright, her hand to her mouth, the tears running down her cheeks. Seeing how upset she was, the Prince leapt to his feet at once to stop the play, but before he could do so, she put a hand on his arm.

"Let them go on, dearest," she whispered to him. "I want to see it all, the whole play."

At that moment, in through the great doors there came three camels, masked puppeteers inside them. Living, breathing creatures they were, their heads tossing against their bridles, their tails whisking, chewing and grunting as they came, and each of them ridden by a king bearing gifts.

The goose woke up suddenly, not at all pleased at this unwelcome intrusion. He prowled and hissed around the three kings, head lowered, wings outstretched, as they presented their gifts to Mary and the baby. Then, hissing like a dozen angry snakes, he turned on the camels and chased them off into the night, the three kings running helter-skelter after them. Laughter and clapping filled the hall. The goose took a bow, and then went to have a look at the baby, before settling down again to sleep beside the sheep and the goat and the cow.

Just then, who should come in but several shepherds, looking a bit lost and bewildered. The goose slept on, for the moment. The shepherds found the baby and knelt before him to worship him. Then they sang a carol to him, a lullaby:

"Hush my babe, lie still in slumber,
Holy angel guard thy bed,
Sweetest blessings without number,
Gently fall upon thy head."

As they sang, the Prince saw the Princess was crying still. Then, like a sudden miracle, she was smiling, smiling through her tears. And by the time the goose woke up, saw the shepherds and proceeded to chase them, around and around the great hall, she was on her feet and crying again, but with laughter this time.

"I love that goose!" she cried. "I love that goose!"

Everyone was on their feet now, clapping and cheering as the puppeteers came forward to take their bow. The applause went on and on, because everyone could see that the Princess too was clapping and laughing with them, her eyes bright again with life. It was many minutes before the hall had quietened and the Prince could speak.

"You have made my Princess smile," he told the players. "You have made her laugh. So, as I promised, my kingdom is yours."

One by one, the players took off their masks, and then the Prince knew them for who they were, that same family of travellers who had sheltered him from the snowstorm, to whom he had told his story.

"We do not want your kingdom," said the old grandfather. "We wanted only to be sure your story had a happy ending, that the Princess could learn to smile again. And now she has. It will soon be the best of times again for her, and for all of you in this happy land."

"Then at least, stay with us a while, stay for our feasting," said the Prince, "so that in some small way I can repay your kindliness and hospitality."

So the players stayed, and feasted, but they would not stay the night. "Travellers," said the old grandfather, as he climbed up into their caravan, "never stay for long. We like to keep travelling on. We just follow the bend in the road. But before we go, we should like to leave you a Christmas gift. Our little goose. We've talked to him about it. He says he's quite happy to live in a palace – just so long as you don't eat him!" And so, leaving the goose behind them, they went on their way into the night. No one knew where they had come from. No on knew where they went. No one ever saw them again.

By Christmas time the next year, Princess Serafina was not only restored to full health and happiness, but she had her own precious baby in her arms, which, of course, was just what the Princess had been longing for all this time. In the play they put on in the great hall that Christmas, the Princess played Mary, and her own child played the baby, kicking his little legs and waving his fists just as he should.

The goose, of course, still insisted on playing the goose. He wasn't the kind of goose you could argue with, everyone knew that. And in his honour – just in case he ever found out – no one in the land ate roast goose at Christmas ever again.

Huff

Written by Wendy Cope
Illustration by Sholto Walker

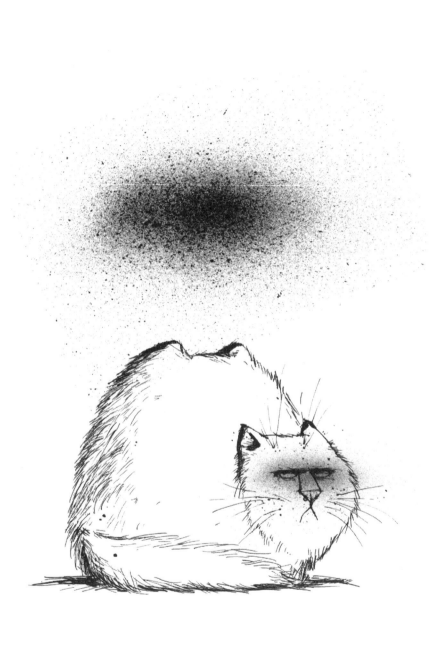

I am in a tremendous huff –
Really, really bad.
It isn't any ordinary huff –
It's one of the best I've had.

I plan to keep it up for a month
Or maybe for a year
And you needn't think you can make me smile
Or talk to you. No fear.

I can do without you and her and them –
Too late to make amends.
I'll think deep thoughts on my own for a while,
Then find some better friends.

And they'll be wise and kind and good
And bright enough to see
That they should behave with proper respect
Towards somebody like me.

I do like being in a huff –
Cold fury is so heady.
I've been like this for half an hour
And it's cheered me up already.

Perhaps I'll give them another chance,
Now I'm feeling stronger
But they'd better watch out – my next big huff
Could last much, much, much longer.

The Double Eagle Has Landed

Written by Anthony Horowitz
Illustration by Romi Caron

T here was just one question I had to ask myself. How could I have ended up, dangling from a flag pole, twelve storeys above a street in East London, with an armed maniac walking towards me, a rabid dog snapping at my fingertips and the world's worst detective clinging to my ankles? Actually, a second question also came to mind. What was I going to do next?

It had all started earlier that same day … a damp, wet, Tuesday in January, the sort of day that made you forget that Christmas had ever happened or that spring would ever come. Looking out of the window, all I could see was rain. In fact, looking into the window, I could see quite a bit of rain too. The roof was leaking. My big brother, Tim, was sitting behind his desk with water dripping into a bucket beside him. The bucket looked happier than him.

You may have heard of Tim Diamond. He called himself a private detective. That was what it said on his business card … at least, it did if you ignored the spelling mistakes. He was twenty-five years old, dark-haired and good-looking provided you didn't look too closely. Tim had spent three years as a policeman. In all that time he never prevented a single crime or arrested a single criminal. The truth was, he wasn't too bright. He once put together an Identikit picture of someone suspected of robbing a bank and the police spent the next six months looking for a bald Nigerian with no nose and three eyes. He did once rescue a woman from drowning but she wasn't too grateful. He'd just pushed her in.

After that he set up his own business with an office in Camden Town. He got the place at a knockdown price which was hardly surprising as knocking down was all it was good for. There was a reception room and a kitchen, two bedrooms and a bathroom. The pipes gurgled, the floorboards creaked, the windows rattled and the radiators groaned. On a bad day, you had to shout to make yourself heard. He got a sign painted on the front door. It read: TIM DIAMOND, PRIVATE DETECTIVE and it looked great although in my view it might have been more effective on the outside. Still, at least it reminded him who he was every time he left.

To be fair, Tim did get a few cases and you may have read about them in a series of bestselling adventures such as The Falcon's Malteser, Public Enemy Number Two and South by South East. OK – that's an advertisement but Tim gets five percent from the publishers and frankly he needs it. The last time I looked he was down to his last fifty dollars – and we're not even talking American. I'm still not sure what he was doing with a Zimbabwe banknote in his wallet. It wasn't as if he'd ever been there. But that was all he had and fifty Zimbabwe dollars wouldn't be enough to buy us breakfast … unless we went halves on the egg.

And how did I end up living with him? It was a question I'd asked myself a hundred times and I still hadn't got a sensible answer. I'd moved in when I was thirteen, just after my parents had emigrated to Australia. I've got nothing against the Australians and their dollars are actually worth the paper they're printed on – but I didn't want to leave London and so I slipped off the plane just before it taxied onto the runway. After that it was a choice between living rough and homeless on the streets, begging off passers-by and trying to avoid being arrested and sent to an orphanage. Or moving in with Tim. I'm still not sure I made the right choice.

Anyway, it was my first week back at school and I hadn't had a lot of fun. Either I was growing or my uniform had shrunk in the wash … if this went on much longer I'd soon be back in shorts. And of course, I was the only person in the school who hadn't got a new X-box or a new i-Phone or any other expensive gadget with a letter in front of it. Tim wouldn't even have been able to afford a new T-cup and although mum and dad had sent me a card from Sydney (Santa surfing on Bondi Beach) they'd forgotten to enclose the book token or, better still, the cheque. On the other hand, I knew that things were tight out there. My dad had started a new business selling heated toilet seats but apparently the bottom had fallen out of the market.

So I was in a bad mood when I trudged home that Tuesday afternoon. However, as I climbed the stairs, I heard voices and realised that the miracle of Christmas had finally happened, even if it was a few weeks late. Tim had a client!

I let myself in and sure enough, there was my big brother, leaning across his desk with the wobbly half-smile he used when he was trying to look professional. The man sitting opposite him was big and fat. He must have weighed three hundred pounds and my first thought was that I hoped he'd chosen the right chair. He had ginger hair, a round face and a big smile although with that hair and that face I wouldn't have thought he had a lot to smile about. He was wearing a crumpled suit and a tie that had only just made it all the way round his neck. There was a scarf draped across his shoulders and leather gloves on his hands. It seemed strange that he hadn't bothered to take them off although it was a cold day outside. I guessed he was in his late thirties and if he didn't give up the crisps and the sugary drinks, forty was going to be a stretch. He was smoking a cigarette which wouldn't help either. He either needed to see a doctor or an undertaker … it was just a question of which one would get to him first.

Tim saw me come in. He was obviously in a good mood because he didn't try to throw me out. "This is Mr Hollywood," he said.

"Underwood," the man corrected him. "My name is Charles Underwood. And who are you?"

"I'm Nick Diamond," I said. I jerked a thumb at Tim. "I'm his brother."

"Mr Thunderwood needs a private detective," Tim explained. "He was just saying that he needs someone reliable and responsible … someone who isn't afraid of danger."

"Then what's he doing here?" I asked.

"I got your brother's name out of the telephone book," Underwood replied. He looked for an ash-tray. There wasn't one so he stubbed the cigarette out on the desk. "I have an office in Clerkenwell," he went on. "It's on the twelfth floor of the House of Gold." He waved a hand in the air. "That's what I do for a living, Mr Diamond."

"What? You're a conductor?"

"No. I buy and sell gold. Mainly old coins. Right now I have a Double Eagle in my safe worth five million pounds."

Tim's mouth dropped. "Your safe is worth five million pounds?"

"No. The Double Eagle is worth five million pounds."

"What? And it's guarding the coins?"

"The Double Eagle is the gold coin, Mr Diamond. It was made in America 1933 and it's incredibly rare." Underwood leaned forward – as far as his stomach would let him. "It landed in London yesterday … it was flown in from Chicago. And now I've had a tip-off that someone is planning to steal it. That's why I need a private detective."

"Why don't you just move the coin?" I asked.

"That was my first thought. But it's too risky. If I walked out of the office with the coin in my pocket, someone could shoot me or stab me or run me over …"

"They could do all three!" Tim exclaimed.

"That's right. It would be easy to steal it off me. The coin is safer where it is …"

"In the safe," Tim muttered. "But is it a safe safe?"

"It's six inches thick," Underwood replied. "It has a thirty-digit code. The office is locked with a sophisticated alarm system and the building is patrolled day and night. But here's the problem. The man in charge of security – his name is Harry King – he's the man who's planning to rob me. He's going to break in at midnight tonight."

"How do you know?" I asked.

"I'll tell you." Underwood took out another cigarette and rolled it between his fingers. It wasn't easy because he was still wearing the gloves. "First of all, King is a bad sort. I've checked him out. He spent three years in prison."

"He was a guard?" Tim asked.

"No. He was a prisoner. Armed robbery. Of course, you might think he's reformed. I'm all for giving a man a second chance. But the other day I overheard him talking on his mobile phone." Underwood lit the cigarette. Grey smoke curled out of his lips. I was just glad I wasn't one of his lungs. "Even before I found out about his past, I never trusted King," he went on. "He's a sleazy sort of fellow, always short of money.

I think he gambles. I hate people who gamble!"

"I bet you do," Tim agreed.

"Anyway, he was standing outside the building with that dog of his –
he has an Alsatian – talking on the telephone."

"Wait a minute. Wait a minute," Tim interrupted. "How could the
dog talk on the telephone?"

"King was the one talking," Underwood growled, doing a pretty
good impersonation of the dog himself. "I heard him say that he'd go in
at twelve tonight. He said he would get it and hand it over tomorrow."

"How do you know he was talking about the coin?" I asked.

"I don't. I can't be a hundred percent certain. And that's why I
haven't gone to the police. Let's call it a hunch. I just don't think he
adds up."

"He's bad at maths?" Tim asked.

Underwood ignored him. "I want you to go to the building tonight,"
he went on. "I can give you a key to the front door. I want you to follow
King and see what he gets up to. My office is number 1205. If he goes
anywhere near it, you call me or you call the police. Tomorrow morning
I have a dealer coming to buy the coin. I just need to be sure it's still
there …"

"All right, Mr Slumberwood," Tim said. "I'll do it. But it's going
to cost you seventy pounds."

"I'll pay you twice that to make sure the Eagle is safe!"

"OK. A hundred and twenty pounds it is."

"I'll give you the money tomorrow." Underwood got to his feet and
I almost felt the chair sigh with relief. He slid a plastic entry card onto
the desk. "This is an electronic key-card," he said. "It'll get you into the
main building. The House of Gold is on St John's Street. You can't miss it."

"Why is that?" Tim asked.

"Well … it's got HOUSE OF GOLD written on the front door."

"Good."

"And make sure Harry King doesn't spot you! I don't want him
to know we're onto him."

"I'm the invisible man," Tim said. "Everyone who sees me calls me that!"

Underwood was about to leave but before he went he did something very strange. He picked up the dead butts from the cigarettes he'd smoked and slid them into his top pocket. Why would he do something like that? He didn't look like the sort of man who was interested in keeping the place clean. Of course, Tim hadn't even noticed. He was already imagining the money he was going to be paid the next day. And that worried me too. If Underwood had a five million pound coin that he was going to sell, how come he couldn't afford even a five pound down payment now?

"Tim," I said, once he'd left. "I've got a bad feeling about this."

"Relax, kid!" Tim winked at me. "This case is right up my street."

"Yeah. The street to the loony bin," I thought. But I didn't say that. "I'm not so sure I trust this guy Underwood," I went on. "That story he told you … the security guard talking about the robbery on his phone. Don't you think that's a bit unlikely?"

"Not really. Lots of security guards have phones."

"I mean, talking about a robbery when he can be overheard! Also, he didn't pay you. And he told you to ring him if anything happened but he didn't give you a number!"

"Look, Nick," Tim interrupted. "It's a simple job. All I have to do is follow the security guard and see what he gets up to."

"OK," I said. I knew I was going to regret this but I felt I had no choice. "But I'm going too."

"Where are you going to?" Tim asked.

"I'm coming with you, Tim."

"Forget it, Nick. No way. Absolutely not. No chance."

"So when do we leave?" I asked.

Tim nodded. "As soon as it's dark."

***

The House of Gold might have had a fancy name but it was just an ordinary office building in an ordinary street. It was twelve storeys high with a flagpole sticking out below the roof and as I glanced up at it for the first time, I never thought that in about half an hour's time, I was going to be clinging to it with both hands with Tim clinging to me by both ankles. But maybe that's my problem. I just don't have enough imagination.

We let ourselves in using Underwood's card and to be honest, part of me was surprised that it even activated the doors. I'd thought it was going to be as fake as him. We found ourselves in a reception area with half a dozen potted plants that looked half-dead and wilting … which was quite surprising as they were actually made of plastic. There was an empty reception desk and on the wall a list of names. More than fifty jewellers and gold dealers worked at the House of Gold and there was the name, Underwood, with the number 1205 – among them. That surprised me too. Charles Underwood hadn't looked like a coin dealer to me. Everything about him had smelled wrong … even his aftershave.

There was no sign of Harry King or his dog but that was just as well. I had no desire to get arrested or bitten … and who knows? If he'd seen us Harry might have done both.

Tim was wearing black jeans, a black jersey and a black balaclava covering his face. Frankly, he looked more like a burglar than a private detective and more like an Alpine skier than either. I was still wearing my school clothes. Tim had a torch but he didn't need it because there were lights on throughout the building. Anyway, the batteries were dead and it occurred to me that any minute now we could be too. I had a nasty feeling about this. Half of me wished we hadn't come and the other half agreed.

"There's a lift!" Tim waved his torch in the direction of a corridor leading away from the reception area.

"Forget it, Tim," I said. "We can't risk it."

"What? You think it might break down?"

"No. But somebody might notice it moving. Let's take the stairs."

We found the staircase and began the long climb up. There were sixteen steps between each floor and twelve floors. I counted every one of them. Finally, we got to the top and found ourselves in front of a pair of solid-looking swing doors that met in the middle with metal plates and wires positioned so that they connected. It was like the entrance to a vault or to a top secret laboratory or something. I stopped to catch my breath. Perhaps we should have taken the lift after all.

"Tim ..." I began.

"What?"

"I'm not sure you should open these doors."

"Why not?"

Tim pushed them open. At once about a hundred bells all around the building began a deafening clang. A recorded voice burst out of hidden speakers shouting "Intruder Alert! Intruder Alert!" Somewhere, a dog started howling. Searchlights positioned in the street exploded into life, blasting the windows, blinding us. In the far distance, about fifty police cars turned on their sirens, shattering the still of the night as they began to close in.

"Do you think the doors are alarmed?" Tim asked.

I grabbed hold of him and began to drag him back down the stairs. All I knew was that this was the sophisticated alarm system that Underwood had mentioned and we had to get out fast. If the police arrived, how were we going to persuade them that we weren't actually trying to rob the place ourselves? But I'd only taken two steps before I realised that the howling was coming from below me and about half a second later, the biggest dog I had ever seen turned the corner and began to bound towards us.

By big – I mean big ... perhaps a hundred pounds of knotted muscle and fur. Its eyes were ablaze and the last time I'd seen so many teeth I was looking at a crocodile. It was leaping towards us with a look in its eyes that simply said "dinner" – and it was clear that Tim and I were the ones on the menu. Behind it, I glimpsed a uniformed figure who I guessed must be Harry King. He was black and bald with arms and shoulders you could use to advertise a gym. Frankly, I've seen friendlier sumo wrestlers. He was about ten steps behind the dog. They were both heading our way.

"This way, Tim!" I shouted.

We burst through the double doors. It was too late to do any more damage. The alarms were still jangling and the recorded voice was louder than ever. "Intruder Alert!" I think we'd got the message. The police cars were getting nearer too. It was like the whole building was under attack. I was already wishing I'd stayed at home. I'd left behind two hours of French homework – but even that would have been more fun than this.

We found ourselves in a long, dark corridor with offices on both sides. One of them had to be 1205 but I didn't stop to check the numbers. I was thinking of the dog heading our way. The doors had swung shut behind us and that might hold it up for a moment. But a moment wasn't long enough. What was I looking for? A second staircase. A lift. A fire escape. A helicopter launch pad with a helicopter just about to take off. Anything to get us out of here.

"In here!" Tim had found a door and burst through it. I didn't bother following him. With typical brilliance, he had found his way into the gent's toilet. I waited for him to come out again and at that moment the double doors burst open and the dog came pounding through. Tim was holding something and hurled it in the dog's direction and at least that distracted it for a few seconds. In the meantime, I found another door. This one opened onto a staircase that climbed up. We took it. We had nowhere else to go.

The staircase led to a door which took us onto the roof and before we knew what had happened we were out beneath the stars with a freezing January breeze whistling around us, reminding us we'd be much warmer inside. Unfortunately, Fido was also inside and given a choice between catching a slight cold and being ripped to pieces, I knew which I preferred. Without even stopping to catch breath, we set off across the roof. Surely there had to be another way down.

Then two things happened at once. The dog burst through the same door that we'd just taken. That was when I realised it was rabid. White foam was pouring out of its mouth and its eyes were bulging and discoloured. At the same time, Harry King appeared. I wasn't sure where he had come from but he was suddenly there, making his way towards us, and he was holding something in his hand. He raised it, pointing it in our direction.

"It's a gun!" Tim shouted.

To be fair to him, he was trying to protect me. I mention this only because it was Tim who nearly killed me. Thinking that Harry was about to fire, he rugby-tackled me to the ground. The only trouble was that there was no ground. At that moment, we were right on the edge of the building and with a certain sense of surprise I realised that, in his attempt to protect me, my big brother had just thrown me into thin air with a twelve-storey fall and a concrete pavement waiting for me below. I was also aware that Tim was coming with me. I don't quite know why but part of me was glad that we were going to be together at the very end. This seemed an unusually stupid way to die, even by Tim's standards. I'd have hated to do it on my own.

But we didn't die. You've probably guessed what happened next. I saw the flag pole and managed to grab hold of it and at the same time, Tim managed to grab hold of me. And that's how this all started (you can go back to the beginning if you've forgotten) with the two of us dangling in the air like a couple of comedians in those old black and white movies except without the honky tonk piano and the laughing audience.

I don't think I'd have been able to hold on for more than about thirty seconds. My hands felt like they were being pulled off my wrists. My feet felt like they were being pulled off my ankles. My shoulder blades and spine weren't doing too well either. Looking down, I could just make out my big brother, swaying in the breeze. And looking up …?

Well, suddenly Harry King was there, leaning over the edge. The dog was with him. But neither of them was trying to kill us.

"Hold on!" Harry shouted. He lay on his stomach and reached down with one hand and I felt his fingers close around my wrist. I could tell at once that he was incredibly strong. It was like being seized by a crane. And then, inch by inch, he was pulling me up – and Tim with me. My fingers found a grip on the edge of the building and I was able to help him, pulling myself over the top. At the same time, Harry got a stronger grip under my arms. He was panting with the effort. The dog – still foaming at the mouth – was wagging its tail. This was all very strange. We weren't being chased any more. We were being saved.

I felt solid ground underneath my chest, then my thighs as I was pulled onto the roof. Tim came with me. As soon as I was safe, Harry reached past and helped him up the rest of the way. Down below, I could hear the police cars pulling in. There was the thud of car doors and feet hitting the pavement. Somehow I knew that the ordeal was almost over. But I still didn't quite know what it was all about.

"Are you OK?" Harry demanded. Looking at him close up, I could see that he was a friendly, pleasant sort of man. But then he had just saved my life which may have helped change my opinion. He certainly wasn't carrying a gun. What Tim had seen was actually a walkie-talkie … and it made my head spin to think that this had been enough for him to throw both of us over the edge of a twelve-storey building.

"Thanks," I muttered.

"Who are you? What are you doing here?"

I didn't answer. Too much had happened too quickly. Then the first police made it up onto the roof and I was almost grateful when we were both placed under arrest.

***

There's not a great deal more to tell.

I suppose I should start with the man who had come to the office and who had told us his name was Charles Underwood. It wasn't. The real Charles Underwood visited us in our cell and he turned out to be silver-haired, about five foot three and Irish. He wasn't very happy either. Because while Harry King had been chasing us, while the police had rushed up to the roof and arrested us, someone had slipped into his office and stolen his precious Double Eagle coin.

I only had to explain it all to Tim five or six times before he understood. The fake Underwood was the thief. Somehow he'd got a key to the building – which he'd given to us – but he hadn't been able to get past the security system in order to crack the safe. So he'd used us as a diversion. We'd been spotted by CCTV cameras the moment we entered – that was how the police had got there so quickly. We'd set off the alarms. We'd been chased onto the roof. And while everyone was busy dealing with us, he'd had ample time to open the safe and make off with the contents.

And while I'm tying up the loose ends, I might as well mention that Harry King had never been in prison and his dog, Lucy, didn't have rabies. When Tim had ducked into the men's toilet, he had picked up a bar of soap and that was what he had thrown as we ran for the stairs. The dog had eaten the soap – and that was why it was foaming at the mouth.

They never did find the thief. Of course, we gave the police a description but the man who had come to our office could have been wearing a wig. He could have had padding under his jacket. He must have heard about Tim from somewhere because it can't just have been luck that had made him choose the most stupid detective in London. Tim had played right into his hands. And of course those hands were wrapped in gloves so although the police searched our office, they didn't find so much as a fingerprint. Our visitor had been careful to take his cigarette butts with him too – making sure he left no DNA.

He was one of the ones who got away but that's what happens now and then. In fact, where Tim Diamond is concerned, it happens quite a lot of the time. A happy ending? Well – I hadn't been killed. I hadn't fallen twelve storeys and fractured every bone in my body. I hadn't been chewed up by the dog. And speaking personally, I was perfectly happy with that.

Endings

Written by Michael Jecks
Illustrations by Andrew Joyce

H e had endured, if that was the right word, far too long.
"No more food. I'm too tired."
"Sir, you must eat."

Sir Baldwin de Furnshill let his head sink back on the cushion and closed his eyes. He need not eat. He wanted death. He had nothing to live for in this, the forty-second glorious year of the reign of King Edward III of England and of France.

When young, Baldwin had joined the crusading army sent to defend Acre from the Mameluke hordes. He had no thoughts of living to ninety five in those days. Ninety-five! Such an age!

There, in the Holy Land, he had thrown himself into the fighting. He was not far from William de Beaujeu, Grand Master of the Templars, when that noble knight was struck and had to be dragged from the battle, declaring he was dead, and exhorting his men to fight on, and the Templars were inspired to ever greater acts of courage and self-sacrifice.

But yet the Kingdom of Jerusalem was lost. The city fell, and even as Baldwin sailed away on one of the last ships to leave the port, he could see the smoke rising where the last of the men were making their stand. Within days, the Christians were all slaughtered or enslaved. Their example of self-sacrifice at Acre was the reason why Baldwin had joined the Knights Templar in the first place. He had been proud to be accepted into the order, a warrior monk.

It was because of the failure of the Templars to defend the Kingdom of Jerusalem that the King of France and Pope conspired against them.

These two knew that the people of France would believe any crimes levelled against the order, for how could God have allowed His lands to fall into the hands of wicked heathens, had not His warriors been unworthy. They must have been guilty of especially foul offences to have so upset Him.

In the tumult of those days, with forecasts of the end of the world, of famine, war and plague, it was easy for people to blame one group. The Templars were captured and tortured even as their shattered order tried to renew their strength for a new crusade. It was too late. The

French King arrested all Templars on that accursed day, Friday October thirteenth, and destroyed them utterly. Broken, tortured, executed, there were few like Baldwin who survived without injury.

The fears of Christians were soon proved only too well justified. So many died in the famines of thirteen fifteen and sixteen that there were scarce enough men to plough the fields. Then came the plague, that awful, God-given scourge of all men. Baldwin's wife and daughter both died in that first immolation, God rest their poor souls. He missed them every day, every single day.

His friend, Simon, he too was dead. For all that he had been younger than Baldwin, he had succumbed to a splinter. All men feared such pricks: within a few days it had been necessary to drain some pus, then his hand began to lose feeling and grew green and foul, before the gangrene set in properly.

Wars, too, had raged up and down England, all through his fifties, followed by the new king's battles with Scotland, and then the expeditions to France, eventually winning the crown there too, thirty-odd years ago.

That was where his boy had died. Squire Baldwin, his son, had been with the King's host at Crecy, and was one of the foolish dead. Trying to catch a friend's terrified horse, he was struck on the side of the head and killed instantly. Only twenty years old, and such a good boy. Such a good man.

That was the end of Baldwin's life, in truth. He had continued serving as Keeper of the King's Peace, occasionally as Justice of Gaol Delivery or as Member of Parliament, but he and Jeanne had found life had lost its savour after Baldwin's death. And since Jeanne's death, only three years after their son's, Baldwin had continued existing, but without pleasure. There could be no pleasure. He awaited death with keen anticipation.

There was a strange noise, and he tilted his head. Voices down below his bedchamber, one raised in expostulation, the other his servant murmuring quietly.

"Who is it?" he demanded. Couldn't they leave him alone even to die in peace?

"It's the Constable of Crediton, Sir Baldwin. I have told him you can't …"

"Am I so decrepit that I can't decide for myself, man?"

"Sir, you are tired. You wouldn't even eat your …"

"Constable, get up here. Now!"

The slow tramp of boots up his staircase, and then the Constable of the town was with him.

"Well?"

"There's a man killed, Sir. We hoped you could come and have a view of him. It looks a little odd, and …"

"Sir Baldwin is too old to go gallivanting about the country."

Baldwin glared. "Sir Baldwin will decide for himself, you great congeon! Get out!"

And he listened carefully to a fresh tale of murder and cruelty, while his servant, concealing his smile of triumph, quietly slipped from the room.